# A Candle for the Children

✦

*Jennifer Zomar*

iUniverse, Inc.
New York   Bloomington

# A Candle for the Children

iUniverse books may be ordered through booksellers or by contacting:

iUniverse
1663 Liberty Drive
Bloomington, IN 47403
www.iuniverse.com
1-800-Authors (1-800-288-4677)

ISBN: 978-0-595-52375-7 (pbk)
ISBN: 978-0-595-62432-4 (ebk)

iUniverse Rev Date 11/18/2008
Printed in the United States of America

For you, Steven. Because
we admire you, believe in
you, and love you.
Thank you for coming to live with us.
Also for Grandma and Grandpa Zomar.

# *Content*

# *Acknowledgments*

Thank you and blessings to Cal Rosner, or rather Gray Wolf's Spirit, who made me realize I would indeed write a book and that it was a story that needed telling.

I would be grossly spiritually negligent if I didn't take this opportunity to acknowledge my "guardian angels." All my life, I have prayed to them, believed in them, and listened for their guidance. Their insistence that I write our story is the strongest influence in my life that I have ever felt, and there was never a question of me not completing this project, regardless of those hesitant times.

Many people have been my readers. Their suggestions on how to improve the book were most appreciated. Victoria Huybers, Kathleen Ariens, Meredyth Albright, and Mary Ann Miller offered encouragement not only to continue with the story, but also to get professional help with it. (Here I go again!) Those suggestions led to my unbelievably good luck in finding J. Jamakaya, an editor who was willing to take on a challenge and agreed to work with me. Her sense of humor and patience were prominent as she guided me throughout the story. I am so grateful for her expertise.

The readers who helped me smooth out the remaining roughness of the story are Pat Cook-Bettiga, Bonnie Burgette, Christine and Greg Porter, Helen Molle, Patrice Wisneski, and Jackie Martin. Thanks to all of you, and especially to those who took the biggest risks and offered the most valuable suggestions.

Lastly, thank you, Benjamin and Steven. Without you, there would be no story.

# *Introduction*

Our infant grandson, Steven, was suffering seizures, and I was becoming worried that he was not going to receive appropriate medical care. His mother told me she had taken the baby to his pediatrician several times, but the doctor kept telling her it was nothing more than colic. Jackie was my confidante. Distraught with my worries and fears, I called her, and she promised that not only would she pray for us, but she would call several of our mutual friends so they could join our prayers for our suffering baby boy.

Within days, she called back to tell me that not only were several friends praying for us, but that several congregations throughout the United States, from our northern home state to as far away as Hawaii, would be saying prayers for Steven and his parents. The friends Jackie had contacted in the first congregation had become responsible for the wonderful prayer chain. They wanted me to understand that they would not necessarily be praying that Steven "get well," but would be praying for "God's will" regarding Steven's health and for the parents to cope with whatever God's will was. It was almost impossible for me to imagine or visualize so many people and congregations praying for my suffering infant grandson, but the comfort and spiritual strength the prayers gave me were one more testament that prayer does help to heal and overcome obstacles.

Although the seizures were eventually controlled, Steven continued to struggle with normal developmental progression, which had been disrupted during the several months he suffered seizure activity. Tragically, his parents neglected to involve him in early childhood interventions, as advised by his doctors. My husband, Benjamin, and I had always been concerned about what we thought should be better parenting. Steven was six years old, and Benjamin and I were at the end of our emotional ropes when we finally came to the conclusion that if we didn't provide a structured, loving environment for him to thrive in, he would never reach whatever potential he was capable of.

Steven had been living with us for three years when our pastor suggested to her congregation that they each light a candle at mealtime for a period of one month and pray for a child who might be suffering in any way. Steven wanted his prayer to be for children who are living in unhappy homes to find happy homes to live in. Since that first candle was lit and the first prayer said, Steven has continued lighting candles and saying prayers for unhappy children at every meal. He never asks if his prayers are getting answered. He remains confident that other children will find happy homes, just as he did.

Because Steven has continuing mental delays, further complicated by autism, he informed me, with his limited verbal skills that I needed to write a book. He wanted his story to be told. He believes his story will be an influence in helping other children secure those happy homes that he prays for every day.

I have prayed and meditated for guidance on how best to tell Steven's story. I decided against a medical angle; there are many books available for those seeking medical understanding of autism. I chose to include several examples of how we work with and teach Steven, but not to make his story a how-to book. I finally decided that Steven's story could be told most effectively as a multigenerational story. It is a story about life's choices—how choices we make affect not only our own lives but also those who love and depend on us.

My objective in telling Steven's story is to give incentive and encouragement to others to make the necessary changes in their lives to provide loving homes for children to flourish in. Too often in our society, as our story will show, problems are accepted as normal, or sufferers don't want help. To tell Steven's story, I have to put aside what little privacy Benjamin and I will have left and jump in, hoping to provoke others to evaluate questionable areas of their lives and to seek appropriate approaches to change what they can change. By exposing myself and those I love, I expect to enrich other lives by offering insights into happiness, stability, and a source of love and guidance that is there for the asking. I hope to encourage readers to open their hearts and homes to children who may be suffering. Most of all, I want to encourage emotional and mental wellness, because if the adults aren't closed off by self-centeredness and self-pity, then, for sure, suffering children will have a chance at love and happiness.

# Chapter 1

## *A New Beginning*

My life as I know it today began on a beautiful, warm March day in 1977. The window in the Alcohol and Other Drug Abuse (AODA) counselor's second-floor office was wide open; the screens hadn't been put on yet. Wonderful spring air filled the room. The counselor sat with his feet on top of the desk in a relaxed fashion. While pacing his office, I noticed the open window and went to it to breathe in some fresh air. Seeing me go to the window, the counselor sprang to his feet. Clearly, he thought I was going to jump out the window. His reaction made me feel powerful.

I was twenty-five years old, and my life was such a mess that I had been legally ordered to receive counseling for alcoholism. I was as angry as a young woman can get! I couldn't believe anyone would think I needed professional help. I was struggling but working hard to get ahead in life. So what if I drank once in a while? It helped me forget my problems. It was everyone else's fault. If other people would stop interfering in my life, maybe I wouldn't drink so much. I should not have been arrested for drunk driving, either. After all, I knew people who drove while more intoxicated than I was, and I didn't see them getting arrested. But after two arrests for "operating while impaired," I needed my driver's license back, and so I had to comply with the counseling order.

By no means was I an easy nut to crack. I put up one heck of a fight, letting them know how unfair it was that they pulled my name out of a hat and decided I needed therapy. Being forced by the system to seek alcoholism counseling, I couldn't contain the anger I felt. I was so angry during my first appointment with the AODA counselor that I couldn't sit in a chair. I paced his office. I kicked at his file cabinets. In my rage, I had enough sense to know I wasn't angry with the counselor himself; I felt as if, along with the legal system, everyone and everything in my entire life was treating me unfairly. I had tremendous pent-up anger I could no longer contain, and having to see an alcoholism counselor was the final straw. Then and there, my rage spewed out.

This counselor made a few more weekly appointments for me and began each session with, "When was the last time you drank?"

Each time, I answered honestly, "Last night."

After all, I wasn't an alcoholic. I could have a couple of drinks. I think I may have been a little sarcastic with him during our sessions and noncompliant with his recommendations, like not drinking for a week. When he refused to work with me, I realized he wasn't going to put up with my sarcasm and bull-headedness. "You little bitch," he said, "find a counselor who will put up with you." No one had ever talked to me like that before! Well, actually, I think they might have, but I was just too darned ditzy to pick up on it. Because the system had some real control over my driving privileges, however, I felt I had to let this man's shocking comments sink in. The counselor recommended a woman named Mary who might be willing to work with me. When I had my first appointment with her, I was calm enough to at least sit in a chair.

Mary began our sessions by explaining that I had to agree not to drink for six months, the length of my legally ordered therapeutic contract. Each week I returned for my next session with Mary, she repeatedly used the word "sobriety." Finally, I asked her what that word meant. She told me it was a period of time that people abstained from using drugs or alcohol.

"*What?*" I responded. "You mean some people actually don't drink anything at all?"

I was into my second month of sessions with Mary before I understood her "no drink" contract. By then, Mary had a better idea of what exactly she was dealing with. I wasn't getting drunk, but I was still "having a few." I still thought that drinking meant getting drunk.

During one session with Mary, I mentioned that a guy named Jack visited me, and we had smoked weed together in the past. But when I offered him some smoke, he said, "No, I can't. I just got back from treatment, and I'm not smoking anymore." I asked Mary about his beard and hair, which I'd noticed for the first time were no longer dull and brittle. She said that consumption of drugs and alcohol can deplete the body of vitamins, and the effects can be noticeable in the hair.

My two drunk driving arrests would not have happened if I hadn't been drinking, but I still wasn't convinced I had a drinking problem. The hair thing had me questioning my own dry, brittle hair, though. I was too young to have hair in the condition it was in. If I had physical evidence that alcohol was harming me, I'd probably believe I had a drinking problem. Once I learned what sobriety meant, I stopped drinking my occasional few drinks, but Mary never said anything about not smoking weed. Thanks to my vanity regarding my hair, I finally decided to give complete sobriety from all drugs and alcohol a try. Within weeks, my co-workers were asking me, "What did you do to your hair? It looks great!" "I quit drinking and doing drugs," I told them.

Alcoholics are people who have problems resulting from when they drink. But if I was an alcoholic, where did it come from? I learned that alcoholism is thought to be hereditary. Mary said that many surveys conducted with twins separated at birth have helped prove this point. Regardless of environmental factors, if one twin drank, usually the other twin did, too, and it was not uncommon that they preferred the same brand of beverage. On the family questionnaire I filled out at the beginning of my counseling, I reported that my parents drank, but I said they had no problems resulting from it. Several months into my counseling sessions with Mary, I still believed that was true. I believed I had grown up in a typical, "normal" family. My father's dad was an alcoholic; this was common knowledge in the family. He was diabetic and took medicine for it, but he still drank. Even we children knew that you don't drink if you are diabetic and you never drink when taking medicine because the alcohol interferes with the medicine. Acknowledging that Grandfather was an alcoholic gave me a starting point in understanding the hereditary factor. Maybe I was an alcoholic. Though Mary still hadn't convinced me that I had a drinking problem, I was holding to the "no drink" contract. Learning about abnormal drinking behaviors and dysfunctional family interactions was becoming interesting to me now, and I began enjoying the counseling sessions. They were opportunities for me to question incidents in my early childhood that had never quite sat right with me.

In our so-called normal family, we were given beer at a very early age. I was six when I began drinking and learned to control the intoxication. One time, my younger brother drank too much and vomited down the heating vent in the floor. He was so off-balance, he was staggering. He was three or four at the time, and Dad chewed him out. "If you can't hold your beer, then you can't drink anymore!" He didn't give my brother any beer to drink for a long time after that. I liked the sensation I got when I drank beer. I enjoyed the lightness I felt when I spread my arms and flew like an airplane. So after my brother's unfortunate incident, I made sure I drank to only a certain level, and when I began feeling queasy I stopped until I felt better.

I found everything I was learning about alcoholism in my counseling sessions so interesting that I talked about it with anyone who would listen. I talked about Dad giving us children alcohol at such young ages with a young man I knew. "Really?" my friend asked. "Why would he do that? Was it to keep you kids quiet?"

My friend's questions stuck in my head. I gave them a lot of thought. During the 1950s, there were different attitudes about alcohol. It wasn't uncommon for adults to give their children sips of their drinks. Well, Dad gave us the *whole* drink. When I thought more about it, I realized it was his reward for good behavior. If we behaved, we were given beer when we asked for it. If he felt we'd been naughty, we didn't get any. We three older children fought over who got to go to the dump or ice fishing with Dad because we knew he would always stop off at a bar and we could drink beer with him.

Mary talked about normal emotional growth being halted with the onset of alcohol consumption. How dare she! That would mean that I had the emotional maturity of a six-year-old child. I had to give that one some thought. By age twelve, I was drinking to produce wonderful periods of amnesia, better known as blackouts. Maybe my emotional growth stopped then. I spent a good portion of my young life wishing I'd get hurt while walking in the woods and end up in a state of amnesia. Then a nice family would find me and raise me in a loving home. Even if my alcohol-induced amnesia lasted for only short periods of time, I blocked out life in my family for at least a little while. Mary and I also discussed how abnormal disciplinary tactics of dysfunctional families can leave emotional scars. I decided to run an incident from my childhood past her. I wanted feedback on it.

As a very small child, I had a problem with constipation. I remember lying across my mother's lap and her giving me enemas. They hurt like hell, and when I screamed and cried, Mom cracked me on the butt and told me to shut up while she finished. That was pretty much the procedure. I was also teased a lot by my older brother and a male cousin who was my brother's age. They were more like brothers than cousins, as this cousin stayed at our home almost every summer and holiday. They teased me until they had me crying, and then they teased me for crying.

When I was four, our families were planning a large family reunion picnic at a neighborhood resort. Dad told me that Uncle Arnold, who always had the newest gadgets and the "better" things in life, would be making a movie of me with his new camera. Dad said he wanted a movie of me having what he referred to as a temper tantrum so I could see how foolish I looked when I cried. The day of the picnic, I determined I was going to be the best little girl they ever saw. I let Mom curl my hair and didn't even argue when she wanted me to wear a frilly little dress. I stayed away from the adults all day, playing house in one of the cottages. Finally, it was getting late, I was tired, and I figured that Dad would have forgotten about the little movie he wanted to make. I went to Mom to find out if we would be going home soon, and Dad grabbed me. He tried teasing me into a tizzy, but I held my ground and wouldn't give him the satisfaction. Then he remembered the enemas. He laid me across his lap and started shoving his finger up my butt. I was mortified! Besides getting the finger up the butt, I knew that my panties would be showing in the movie because I let my mother put that stupid dress on me.

Mom and Uncle Arnold's wife were screaming at Dad and my uncle to stop and leave me alone. I can still remember Dad's cold beer breath as he laughed in my face. Then the ruckus alerted my brother and cousin that there was some fun to be had. They could get in on the action and not even get hollered at. So as I was crying and gasping for air, they threw me on the ground and held me down, then started shoving grass in my mouth. Uncle Arnold got the whole thing on film. He lived in a different city, but the next time he visited us, he brought this delightful little film that was supposed to humiliate me into complete obedience. Everyone was called into our living room to watch the flick. I stood in the back of the room with my feet apart and my arms crossed and defiantly watched every last second of their little movie. There was a lot of whooping and hollering by the male population, young and old, and comments about how stupid I looked when I had a temper tantrum. When it was done, I thought, *Big deal. I'm stronger than you. Look what you had to do to me to get me to cry.* Then I went outside to play.

But it wasn't over. I used that day for the next twenty-one years as my "secret weapon" to protect myself from ever loving or trusting anyone again. When I started liking someone at school or thinking that an adult was pretty cool, I'd bring myself back to that day to feel the hurt and hatred all over again. I reminded myself how those you love and trust will treat you. I had built a very large chip on my shoulder by the time I ended up in therapy. I never told anyone about my secret weapon until I was twenty-five. That's when I told Mary.

She helped me to understand that what had happened was abuse and that as long as I continued using that experience to "protect myself from loving" that I was indeed allowing my tormentors to continue abusing me. She explained that there are people who will hurt us and that we can pull them in like magnets until we learn to trust ourselves. Victims can remain victims. We can keep sending out signals that we think we deserve to be punished. We can keep attracting those who will continue to hurt us.

The real healing began when Mary suggested I talk to Mom and Dad about that terrible day when I was a four-year-old. So right after that session, I drove to my parents' home. Neither of them appeared to have been drinking too much that day. Perfect. Dad was sitting in the dining room, and Mom was also there, folding clothes. I stood in the kitchen and visited with them over the counter that separated the rooms. When I asked if they remembered taking the movie of me having a temper tantrum, Dad turned white and looked as if he wished he could turn to liquid and puddle into the chair. My mother was finally validated though. She spun around, one arm fully extended, pointed her finger at Dad, and screamed, "I told you she'd remember!"

I stood there, in shock, for maybe a minute. None of us said anything. A hardened silence filled the room. Nothing more needed to be said. Their reactions began clearing years of pain, allowing room for healing in me. Indeed, the healing began then. After I walked out of that silent house, I was able to get on with my life with a clearer understanding of trust. I began trusting myself. For however long it took my father to deal with it, he was the one who had to claim the shame and pain that I had been able to dump on the rightful owner.

I hadn't known what to expect when I went to my parents' home to confront them. In fact, I wasn't sure confronting them would resolve anything for me. In my therapy sessions, I was learning about my fears and lack of confidence. I was beginning to trust that what my therapist suggested might in fact work for me. Despite my best efforts at improving my life before therapy, I hadn't made much progress. Now I was being offered new approaches to old problems, and I became more willing to take risks. Facing my childhood abuse without any expectations of outcome changed me. It gave me a sense of having some control over my life. I began to develop some self-worth.

I still wasn't convinced that I had the emotional maturity of a child, but what I understood at the time was that by not allowing myself to love or trust, based on pain I suffered as a little girl, I was allowing a hurt child to continue dictating areas of my life in ways that a little girl would be incapable of understanding. I had to mentally step back and look at four-year-olds I knew. I had to ask myself, "Now which one of these four-year-olds would I trust to make decisions for me?" Doing this little exercise made me see how silly it was to continue trying to protect myself from emotional pain based on a painful childhood experience. Life sometimes involves suffering emotional pain. By trying to avoid it, I was also depriving myself of experiencing true happiness.

Because I never saw my mother or father stagger when they drank, I never thought they drank too much. Dad worked the swing shift at the mill, and as far as I knew, he never missed any days of work. I did recall, however, that when he was on the day shift and had to go in early, we were often awakened by the phone ringing and Mom jumping out of bed, exclaiming, "Get up, Fred! We overslept again!" Dad made a decent wage at the mill, and almost every Friday and Saturday night he played accordion as his second job. I remember that during the 1950s he got thirty dollars for a playing job. That was darn good money then, plus he drank free beer all night. On Sundays he took the family and his accordion to the neighborhood taverns and entertained for free because he knew the neighbors would buy him beer to show their gratitude.

Regardless of the money Dad made, Mom had little money to buy food. We ate a lot of potato soup, sometimes with meat, sometimes without. I remember my mother sitting on the basement steps sobbing when a fifty-pound bag of potatoes went from $2.00 a bag to $2.50. "What am I going to feed my family now?" she wailed. Because we lived in a rural area, Dad was able to compensate by shooting deer out of season, and we ate venison. Mom and Dad argued a lot over the money he was spending in the bars, and every day, just before the evening meal was ready, we children had to call the bars to find him and tell him supper was ready.

The longer my sessions with Mary continued, the more clearly I understood that Dad was an alcoholic. As confusing as it might seem, I had considered him to be a "drunk," because regardless how much he spent on drinking he still had a job, and Mother was able to scrimp out enough to keep the bills paid. I thought alcoholics were skid row bums—homeless and shaking with tremors; their only focus was getting the next drink. As a child, I was told that Dad's father was an alcoholic. I accepted and understood the explanations I received. I was afraid of Grandpa because he was an alcoholic, so I stayed away from him and never got to know him. My mother didn't drink at all until I was ten, but it seemed that once she realized she wouldn't be able to convince Dad to stop drinking, she decided to drink alcohol to get even with him. "I wonder how he will like it when he comes home and I'm drunk," she said. Once she began mimicking his drinking, she never stopped drinking. She drank with Dad, and she drank when he was elsewhere, either at work or whatever. She died when she was fifty-one. Alcohol had consumed her body.

With therapy, I began to understand my own emotional immaturity. Children raised in an alcoholic family quickly learn to keep their emotions in check. In my counseling sessions, I learned about the countless dysfunctional family interactions that prevented normal emotional growth in children, all of which are common in alcoholic families. When I was happy, I was told, "Wipe that smile off your face." When I was sad or crying, I was told, "I'll

7

give you something to cry about." When I excelled in school, I was told, "If Mrs. Brown saw you at home, she wouldn't think you were so smart or nice." When I talked about my goals and ambitions, Dad always said, "You'll never do it!" and then overwhelmed me with reasons why whatever I wanted to do was impossible. My goals were not unrealistic, however; they were simple things, like getting some training or a better education to get a job that paid more than minimum wage.

There is a strong "no talking" rule in alcoholic families: don't talk about the insanity that is going on in your home. But I always had something to say about the dissatisfaction I felt at home. As we children grew older and our parents grew more dependent on alcohol to ease their unhappiness, my older brother became the designated keeper of the no talking rule. If something came back to the family that I had said in public, I was shamed into questioning my intelligence for saying such a thing. "Shame on you, Jennifer!" my mother and brother said so many times that I was soon doubting myself, my self-worth, and anything I thought to be true. When intimidation and shame no longer silenced me, my brother resorted to the only thing he felt would silence me: he squeezed my throat until I shut up. He only had to do this twice. We were teens, and that's when I stopped trying to be heard in that family. I survived by setting my sights on graduating from high school and leaving home. Rules, the rigid conformity, not being allowed to feel and express emotions—all these can manufacture emotionally void, spiritually broken adults.

Before therapy, I knew anger, elation, and how to feel sorry for myself. From early childhood, I was not allowed to express feelings of anger; if I did, there were unpleasant consequences to pay. I was expected to behave and be pleasant at home, and heaven forbid I felt good about succeeding at anything! If I was too happy about an accomplishment, I was accused of showing off or bragging, and nobody likes a braggart. Naturally, no one in my home wanted to listen to Jennifer feeling sorry for herself, either, so that was strongly discouraged, too. With therapy, I was better able to understand the rage I had felt during my encounter with that first alcoholism counselor. But just because I wasn't dealing with the issues I was angry about, they didn't go away. I kept them all bottled up inside, and eventually the rage erupted, often at the most inappropriate time and at someone who was undeserving of it.

As I learned all these things about emotions and came to understand that I was never allowed to feel them while growing up, I slowly allowed myself to experience and identify new emotions. Over and over throughout the day, I asked myself, "What are you feeling right now?" That's how I became acquainted with my emotions, and it took me several years to easily and correctly identify what I was feeling. I was into my third year of recovery when I went to an Alcoholics Anonymous (AA) meeting and talked about the sadness I was feeling. Even when I felt sadness, I found it to be somewhat comforting. I remember saying at that AA meeting, "So this is what it feels like to be sad. Even though it hurts, it's exciting to be able to feel what sad feels like." I was able to feel sad without someone telling me that I had no reason to be sad. Questioning how I felt also got me in touch with my gut—or my intuition—which is how I learned to listen to what it was saying.

Allowing myself to experience these new emotions and having my therapist assure me that it was okay gave me permission to be playful. I didn't have to gauge my feelings according to what others around me were feeling. If someone I cared for was having a rough day, I could feel compassion for them, but I didn't have to stop having a good day myself. I didn't have to feel guilty because they weren't having a good day and I was.

I think any child raised in an alcoholic home soon learns that they cannot confidently rely on the integrity, honesty, or justice of a parent who indulges in drugs or alcohol. My trust in adults was definitely severed with the "humiliate Jennifer into complete obedience" home movie. I realize that this incident from my childhood is small in comparison to what others may have suffered, but the point is that any abuse is capable of causing tremendous emotional pain and consequences. That day taught me that I couldn't trust my father not to hurt me again, nor could I trust my mother to protect me. This was how I learned how I had been affected by alcoholism as a child of an alcoholic.

Continuing my counseling sessions with Mary, I came to realize that I had been drinking alcoholically. At first I wanted to know how I became alcoholic. Who could I blame for this horrible affliction that prevented me from enjoying an occasional beer? Was my alcoholism hereditary and therefore preordained, or had I learned it from my parents? Having the opportunity to discuss my quirks and behaviors with Mary helped me to answer the questions I had about why I was the way that I was. For the first time in my life I was able to talk with someone and get meaningful, realistic answers. Before long, it didn't matter anymore how I became alcoholic. I simply was one. Understanding there wasn't anyone to blame for my alcoholism made it my responsibility to apply myself to my own recovery.

Much of the laughter in my family was centered on the crazy things we said or did while intoxicated. Our bizarre, drunken behaviors were made light of, if not overlooked. On my family counseling questionnaire, I reported that we were a happy family and that we did many things together. We camped, fished, played penny-ante poker at home, and my parents let us children sing into the microphones while Dad played accordion. We made our own entertainment. Yes, we did many things together. And everything we did included drinking. I was allowed to drink as much as I wanted as long as I didn't get sick, and so my drinking resulted in many of those wonderful periods of amnesia. Our family humor was also heavy with sarcasm.

Problem solving is a skill that each family member in a dysfunctional family learns for himself or herself. The few times I asked my mother for advice, she just responded, "I wish I had your problems. Mine wouldn't seem so bad." When I was eight, I asked Dad to help me fix the chain on a bicycle we children shared. All he said was, "Listen. I'm not very healthy, and I am going to die a young man. I won't be around much longer to help you fix things, so you might as well learn to fix your own things yourself now." I did fix the bicycle chain myself, and I never asked him to help me again. I didn't like Dad very much. I eagerly awaited his early death. I was sure our lives would be better once he died. He lived until his early sixties.

Insane behaviors in dysfunctional families often aren't discussed, not even among family members. When I was sixteen, I returned home late one night after spending the evening with my friends. The house was quiet and everyone was in bed. I'd had a good time with my friends, but once I got home, an incredible feeling of despair settled over me. I felt hopeless. "I don't care anymore," I said to myself. "I don't want to live anymore." I got a chair to stand on so that I could reach a box of pills I knew was on a high shelf in the kitchen. The pills, which were small and red, were in a red box that slid out like a box of matches. The box was about three by five inches, about half an inch high. I had no idea what the pills were for, but the box was full. I poured half the box into my hand and swallowed them, then went to bed, knowing I wouldn't have to wake up again. When I woke up the next morning, I couldn't believe it! I felt no aftereffects from those pills! Not drowsy, not happy. And, no, they weren't laxatives. What the heck were they? Why did I wake up after swallowing half a box of unknown pills? I went about my morning routine as usual, just like the rest of the family. As soon as I had a chance, I grabbed a chair to get that box of pills to see if I could figure out what I'd taken. The box was gone! There was never any question, any hint, any mention of missing pills. I searched the whole house, trying to find where my mother could have put that box. I never found it.

Throughout my childhood and adolescence, I had a variety of friends. In high school I had drinking friends and friends I did not drink with. I spent most of my time with my nondrinking friends, who were more fun and didn't have as many problems as the friends who drank. I blended well with all the social classes, from the kids from the wrong side of the track to the kids from wealthy homes. The wealthy kids were the last ones I wanted to spend time with, however; they were the biggest partiers, and every Monday morning they came to school crying about the trouble they'd gotten into with their parents.

When I was eighteen, my doctor gave me a six-month prescription for Ritalin because he thought I was depressed. I loved the stuff! My goodness, did I have the energy. I was working as a waitress in a fast-paced supper club by then, and after work I stayed up all night painting my bedroom walls in psychedelic colors, using a lipstick brush. But the doctor wouldn't refill my prescription. He was afraid I'd get addicted to the Ritalin. I missed those pills, but then I found street speed. It wasn't as good as Ritalin, but I took speed for a while. The pills were called "white crosses" because they were tiny white tablets with lines crisscrossing the top. I noticed that they made my heart pump really hard, so pretty soon I decided to stop taking those pills.

I often went many months without drinking, but my late teens coincided with the hippie era and the sixties drug culture. I was curious about drugs and wanted to experiment. I became violently ill if I smoked just one or two hits of weed after drinking; when partying and hoping to score some weed, I drank soda, just in case. I was rarely offered anything to smoke because I had that clean, naive appearance most dopers didn't trust. Regardless, I still enjoyed myself when I went out, and I was always the designated driver.

By the time I graduated from high school, I had nice clothes and money for airfare to San Diego (and back if I didn't like it there), where I could further feed my curiosity about hippies and drugs. I fluttered between San Diego and Fort Worth for a few years. Drugs were okay in those days, but I preferred alcohol when I wanted to party. Alcohol was always available, whereas drugs weren't. The effects of alcohol were also more predictable than drugs. Marijuana made me feel tired. I had set my goals higher than the life I saw my mother living. I wasn't impressed with the "free love," limited responsibility lifestyle of those in the drug culture, so I returned to my hometown. Always wishing my life were different, I worked eagerly at trying to improve myself. I lacked problem-solving skills, however, and repeatedly found myself in situations I didn't know how to resolve. Around and around I always went, never making any noticeable improvements in my life.

When I was a senior in high school and during the next couple of years, I had several proposals of marriage, most of them from really nice guys who wanted to take me out of the hellhole they saw me living in. I was told many times that I had "such great potential," and there were men wanting to help me reach it, but my low self-worth and lack of trust made it easy to say no to the proposals. Then Stan came into my life, and when he asked me to marry him, I thought, *Why not? Everyone else is getting married.* Besides, Stan and

I had something in common that the others didn't have—we both liked to drink beer. Stan and I were twenty-one when we married; within a year, our son, Matthew, was born.

And I was so unhappy! At age twenty-three, I went to a doctor and requested a prescription for Ritalin to pull me out of my deep depression. After I explained that the drug had helped get me through a depression once before, the doctor reluctantly gave me a prescription for a few months. But this time, the Ritalin didn't give me the energy-enhancing effect I'd gotten in the past. Believing it would eventually help, I continued to take it anyway.

The combination of Ritalin and alcohol gave me quite a scare one day. My older brother, his wife, and their small children were visiting from the city and staying at our parents' home. Stan, Matthew, and I stayed there overnight, too, as we were planning to do what our family always did together: drink. I didn't drink much that night, but the combination of Ritalin and beer obviously had a negative effect. I awoke the next morning humming. *Loudly.* I couldn't stop humming! And my brain was hurting; it felt like electricity was snapping through my brain. I could *hear* the electricity snapping in my brain. I stayed in my room for a long time, and when I finally realized I wasn't going to make this feeling go away, I went to the kitchen to find Mom and Cindy, my sister-in-law. The men had all gone somewhere for the day, and the children were playing outside. But I couldn't talk. I couldn't stop the loud humming either. When I sat in a chair, my upper body started rocking slowly back and forth. I didn't want to stop the rocking; it was comforting and relaxing. I could understand everything that was being said, but the only way I could only respond was by shaking my head yes or no.

Mom and Cindy went about the day visiting, including me in the conversation as if nothing was wrong. They poured my coffee for me, and when they decided to visit in the living room, Cindy simply took my hand and walked me in with them. They kept the children outside as much as possible because I couldn't stop that humming and they didn't want to freak them out. When the children came in for lunch, Mom and Cindy put me to bed until the kids went out to play again. That electrical snapping in my brain never stopped. Mom and Cindy thought it would be best if I stayed that night again, and so I went to bed early. I slept soundly, and the next morning, I woke up refreshed. The humming and the snapping were gone. When I went into the kitchen, my mother was washing dishes. I walked up next to her and softly told her that I was okay, adding that although I hadn't been able to stop humming the day before, I had understood everything that was going on around me. Mom nodded her head and whispered, "Okay."

We never talked about that day again.

Years later, when I was in a counselor training program to become an AODA counselor myself, I asked a psychologist working with us trainees about my Ritalin-alcohol experience. He explained that I had been "sitting on the fence" of dropping into either complete insanity or into a functional life. "Obviously," he said, "you fell on the side of the fence that returned you to normalcy, or you wouldn't be sitting here. That's why your mother took you to the doctor." I didn't tell him that I had never gone to a doctor. In fact, when I asked him about it, that was the first time I ever talked about it to anyone.

Where I come from, the common parental philosophy was, "Kids are going to drink. We'd rather have them drink at home." I hear that same philosophy from parents today. Dad wanted us children to drink responsibly, but by that he meant you don't get sick and throw up, stagger, wet your pants, or get into fights. The truth is, if I hadn't been given alcohol at home, I wouldn't have missed it. I really never much cared for the stuff. Oh, it was fun playing airplane when I was young, and later I drank a lot to induce blackouts. During my unhappy first marriage, I resorted to the only coping skill I had been taught: I drank the problems away.

When I was legally ordered to receive alcoholism counseling, I was newly divorced and a single parent of a four-year-old son. Having failed at marriage, I was trying to cope by drinking the pain away. Self-pity drinking was why I had been arrested twice within six months for "operating while impaired." Sundays were difficult days for me; they were also heavy drinking days. Convincing myself that Sundays were family days, and now I had no family to have fun with, I wallowed in self-pity. Ah, the insanity of alcoholism. I had a family: my son. Yet, if I took him to the park, I expected him to play while I sat with my six-pack, watching other families and thinking, "Woe is me."

In therapy, I began to understand that maybe my life would be better if I stopped drinking completely—forget about maybe drinking in the future. It took Mary almost six months of weekly sessions to help me reach this decision. Because my family was not supportive of my decision to stop drinking with them, I had to make a choice: sobriety or continued drinking relationships with them. It was difficult to consider cutting family ties, but I'd been able to glimpse a sober lifestyle, and I found it very appealing. By now, my therapy and I had become the joke of the family. I thought the less they knew what I was doing, the less they would have to ridicule. There was so much to learn about alcoholism and how not only my own drinking, but my entire family's drinking and lifestyle, had contributed to the insane life that I now had a chance to change.

I found recovery and new approaches to life exciting. Near the end of my contract for counseling services, Mary suggested I begin attending AA meetings. I was wet-my-pants scared! By then, fear was one emotion I was able to identify. I had previously avoided facing my fears simply by not doing things that made me feel uncomfortable. Everything that Mary suggested worked well for me, however, and I knew I needed to go to meetings. But I was so afraid. Because she was in recovery and went to AA meetings herself, Mary agreed to meet me in the parking lot and walk in with me. Once I was inside the doors, I couldn't believe it. I knew most of the people there! In fact, I had been out drinking with at least half of them!

Richard Nixon was president when I began attending AA meetings. I had attended perhaps six meetings when I went to a meeting one evening feeling full of gratitude. I told the group that they should listen carefully as I didn't understand why I was feeling so grateful that day. "I may never feel this way again," I said. I then imitated Richard Nixon's voice and said, "I am so grateful to the government and for the impaired driving laws, because I got help." I have never lost that feeling of gratitude.

When I began attending AA meetings, I was no longer welcome in my parents' home. If I wasn't going to drink with them, they didn't want me there: "Who do you think you are?" they asked me. "You think you're better than us?" They were not supportive of my efforts to change my lifestyle; in fact, they were a detriment. As difficult as it was, I knew I had to let them go so I could discover who I was. In the past, they had been my only source of love and support, limited as it was. In letting them go, I found an abundance of love and support, often from mere acquaintances. Some of these people were more supportive of my goals and achievements than my family could ever be.

Many children who are raised in alcoholic homes often have other areas of their lives that are more normal. I have found that to be true in my life, too. In some respects, I had a happy, normal childhood. My brothers and I played with the boys next door. We built forts and clubhouses. We played hide-and-seek. We lived in forests and were always exploring. There was a pond adjacent to our parents' properties, and most of our summer days were spent swimming from noon until sunset.

When I was ten, I finally got the sister I'd always prayed for, then another sister arrived two years later. Because of the care I gave to my first sister, from the age of ten, I became the neighborhood babysitter. I also began cleaning two homes on a weekly basis. I made good money. Then Dad decided that as long as I was making such good money, I could buy my own clothes. For the next two years, I still got a yearly swimsuit and a winter coat, and Mom made Dad pop for my Christmas sweater and underwear. The rest was my responsibility. Buying my own clothes made me a smart shopper. I also wanted things I couldn't afford, of course, and I learned how to sew those things. I've made extra money throughout my life by sewing wedding dresses, bridesmaids' dresses, adaptive clothing for children with disabilities, and quilts. When I was sixteen, I got my first "real" job, washing dishes in the supper club where I later waitressed. Once I had a real job, Dad started charging me ten dollars a week for rent. Although parents charging rent wasn't common in those days, it wasn't unheard of, either. It was a way some parents taught their children to make part of their earnings available for living expenses. I learned to budget my money, plus save some in case Dad suddenly died (like he kept promising) or if Mom ever left the bastard, I would have enough to step in and take care of her.

There is a saying in recovery communities, "In order to keep it, you have to give it away." This means that the more individuals in recovery learn about their diseases, and the happier they become, to keep that happiness and wisdom they have to give it away to others. They have to talk about it, and the most appropriate place to "give it away" is at AA support groups. Giving it away is good advice for those who want to stay sober. Those who haven't given it away usually find themselves on another bender, angry and bitter, not knowing what happened. Gradually, each person learns when and how to give it away outside the recovery community. I have found this advice to be true in my own life. The more smiles we give others, the more smiles we get back. It's that simple. The more kindness we offer, the more we are given in return.

I want to be careful, however, about giving the impression that all we have to do is be kind and giving and the world will treat us well. Children who grow up in dysfunctional families are often very kind and giving. They had to be, just to survive. I had to be pleasant and kind to my parents and not ask questions; there were consequences for being disrespectful. Giving others what I assumed they wanted rather than considering what I wanted was what I learned from my alcoholic parents. The kind of giving in my alcoholic home is what made me bitter and angry. It was only with therapy that I learned the real difference between being kind and doing kind things. It was at AA meetings where I learned how to give my good feelings away and trust that I would get more in return.

When making changes in my life, I learned that I have to make these changes without expectations. I gave up destructive behaviors because I knew they were bad for me and that my life would improve. I didn't know what changes to even hope for, and I wasn't expecting any specific changes to result from my sobriety. I simply trusted that if I stayed sober, the overall quality of my life would improve.

I learned that to attain and sustain a happy life, I had to accept life on its terms. I had to trust in God, in his will, not mine. What's wrong with believing that our lives will unfold just as they should? What's wrong with thinking that perhaps God has a better plan in mind for us than what we ever could have imagined? I have found that living my life in a way that makes me feel comfortable with who I am, without expecting rewards for good behavior, has been both exciting and fulfilling.

This is not to say that life after recovery was easy. I expect there will always be challenges. That's life. The difference is that God, friends, faith, and prayer are the sources of strength that pull me through the rough times. One thing is certain: I don't know how I could have made it through life's continuing ups and downs after sobriety without the emotional support of those warm and generous people I met at meetings of AA and Al-Anon (the support group for family members or others who love an alcoholic).

With Mary's help, I didn't set myself up for disappointment and failure by expecting life to flow easily just because I was in recovery. I knew there would be more challenges and disappointments, but I trusted God not to give me more than I could handle. I'll admit there were times when I thought, *He is testing my will and determination*. Raising a son as a single parent also brought many challenges, but it wasn't so much just being a single parent as it was the complexity of his personality. Little did I know that the challenges would extend beyond Matthew into the next generation, and when I thought I was done with my child-raising years, they were in fact only beginning.

# Chapter 2

## *Tested Faith*

All my life I thought critically of my mother for staying with Dad. He was a drunken philanderer who did not provide well for his family. One morning, after lying in bed at night, listening to yet another argument about who Dad was messing around with and listening to Mom cry into the wee hours, I asked her why she stayed with him. She slapped my face so hard I thought my head was going to fly off my shoulders. Okay. I won't ask any more. I was about fourteen at the time. But I always kept my money budgeted in case she ever came to her senses.

Trying to cope with my own unhappy marriage, I had gotten that prescription for Ritalin, but after my harrowing experience with the drug and alcohol combination, I never took another one. I didn't drink any alcohol for several months, either. I tried to make my marriage work; I felt it was important that Stan and I raise our child together. With my mind free from drugs and alcohol, I was able to take a good honest look at our marriage. I had married someone exactly like my dad! Although he didn't drink as much as Dad, Stan was a philanderer. His family owned a landscaping business, and money was readily available—not that he shared much of it with me. At one point in our marriage, in fact, I was down to no underwear, so when I found a bargain at three pair for a buck, I bought them. That evening, while we were driving to a friend's home, I told Stan about my great find. While he was driving the car, he started choking me! He was mad that I'd spent that buck.

Before we got married, Stan and I discussed raising children. It was important to me that I could be a stay-at-home mom, and Stan said there would be no problem with that. Because I love gardening and plants, I could also help out at the nursery. Shortly after the birth of our son, however, Stan came home one evening and told me he had found me a job at a nearby supper club. He said I could start washing dishes until my milk dried up and then take up waiting tables. But I wanted to nurse my baby. I wanted to be home with him. Nevertheless, when Matthew was only nine days old, I went to work washing dishes.

Although I didn't love Stan, divorcing him was very difficult. I always push myself to succeed, and I hadn't entered into that marriage thinking it was for just a little while. We had Matthew to think about, too. I didn't want him to grow up without his father in the picture. Once I mentioned divorce to Stan, however, he was all for it. There wasn't any discussion of the consequences of divorcing; he couldn't get out of there fast enough.

When it came time for one of us to actually move out, Stan let me know that my family was riffraff, that I had come into the marriage with nothing, and I should leave with nothing. That wasn't too difficult. I hadn't brought much into the marriage, and I didn't accumulate much while I was married to him, either. Stan boasted to anyone who would listen that his family's landscaping business was among the top ten local businesses, whereas all I had was an old glass milk bottle that I saved pennies in. This was my secret stash. When I left Stan, I took the milk bottle and Matthew's and my clothes. There was thirteen dollars in that old milk bottle, and that's what I used to start our lives over. I got a job in a nursing home the same day I left my marriage and temporarily moved in with a woman who was also newly divorced.

I worked night shifts so that Matthew would be sleeping while I was away from home, and I nearly killed myself trying to stay awake during the day, trying to share normal days with him. I finally resorted to day-care centers and worked day shifts. From the day I left Stan, I started coping with my feelings of failure by drinking. Luckily for me, I was arrested those two times, within the first year of leaving him.

Quitting drinking is only the beginning of the long road to recovery. I also had to get well physically and mentally. I was grossly immature and fearful of God. I had to learn a whole new way of life. I had to learn to deal with disappointment and joy, find new approaches to solving problems, and learn to just plain live.

Matthew's life didn't seem to be getting any better, even though Mom quit drinking and was doing well in her new life. He was four years old then.

He and I have entirely different personalities: I'm optimistic, he's introverted. I don't mean Matthew is a little bit introverted. I mean he's a whole lot introverted. While I enjoy socializing, he preferred my exclusive attention, and he didn't want me averting my attention from him. When he had my attention, he refused to interact with me in any activities. He seemed to just want me to be focused on him. I was supposed to notice how miserable and unhappy he was, even as he angrily blocked any nurturing or coddling attempts that I made. Even as a toddler, he never willingly sat in my lap and let me read a story to him. I tried coaxing him in many ways. I even tried forcing him. But he just didn't want me to read stories to him. Incredibly, when he was a preschooler, he liked to watch operas on public television. "It's really neat, Mom," he'd say. "They're telling a story."

There were other issues, too. Whereas I took pride in being self-sufficient, Matthew refused to complete any tasks unless he was helped. This ranged from putting his toys into the toy box when he was very young to finishing his homework when he was older. I often sat with him as he did his homework. Sometimes he needed help, other times he didn't, but if I didn't sit there with him, he wouldn't do it. Then, after I struggled with him to finish his homework, he often refused to hand it in. His demands for an adult's exclusive attention were a problem for him at school, too. He refused to participate in classroom discussions or follow instructions on his own, but would easily follow instructions and complete assignments if the teacher sat with him.

The older Matthew got, the less he appeared to pay attention, even with one-on-one help. When he did his math successfully, he refused to complete similar assignments. He seemed to have the attitude that he had already shown me and his teachers that he could do it; why should he have to do it again? I also had problems getting Matthew to follow a set of instructions. I had to tell him the first step and let him complete that before giving him the next step, and so on. He often refused to do the few easy chores I asked him to do, but he never gave me explanations as to why he wouldn't do them. He was developing a negative, angry attitude. In kindergarten, for example, when the other kids clapped after the teacher read a story, Matthew stood up and booed, giving a thumbs-down gesture.

From early childhood, he was skeptical that I knew what I was talking about and worked hard to prove I was wrong when I said anything. He usually pulled it off. When we were getting ready to go somewhere on an absolutely beautiful day, for example, I said, "Oh, look! What a beautiful day! Look at the beautiful, clear blue sky. Not a cloud in the sky." But he looked and looked, then said, "It's cloudy." When I laughed and asked him how he could say such a thing, he pointed to a very small cloud off in the distance. "There's a cloud."

This was pretty much our life. I was either a liar or very stupid. He could always prove me wrong.

In hindsight, I see that my son was obviously suffering from attention deficit disorder (ADD). But he was born in 1973, and we never heard of such a condition back then, so he was merely a perplexing child who needed help and required someone to understand him in the individualized way he was demanding. His teachers and I and anyone else involved with him kept telling him, "Straighten up and behave!" No one recognized that there was something wrong, that he wasn't deliberately being a bad child, and this left him feeling alone, angry, afraid, and hurt. He was treated as if he were naughty and an uncooperative child throughout his entire youth.

Matthew had so many problems, and yet, to help him, I was the one who had to do all the changing. I had to learn to be consistent and punctual. If I said I was going to be somewhere at a specific time, I had to be there. I needed to follow through with discipline. If I told him he'd have a consequence for misbehavior, I couldn't become lax when it was time for him to suffer the promised consequence. No more promising we'd do something fun and then I wouldn't have time for it. I had to learn how to be playful and to have fun with him. But consistency did not come easy for me. Whether or not Matthew was a "problem child," I would have had to learn all these parenting skills. I had been raised by alcoholic parents who lacked loving guidance, and I had learned my parental skills from them. Although as a child I questioned their approaches to discipline or lack of it, before my recovery, I was still only guessing and experimenting with different approaches to parenting. It didn't seem fair, though. I was doing all the right things now. I saw other families making the same changes, and they were getting positive results. Matthew was getting angrier and more uncooperative. My AA support groups helped me to keep going and not to lose faith.

My counselor, Mary, suggested to me early on that perhaps Matthew's life would be better if I placed him with others. That could mean other family members raising him or adopting him out. But rather than allowing me to place Matthew with social services, either my parents or Stan's would have taken over his care. That was the absolutely wrong solution. I never felt that his life would have been any better with either my family or his father's family. Neither set of grandparents was supportive of my attending counseling. They all made jokes to Matthew about my trying to change my lifestyle. Although I was only beginning to learn about dysfunctional families, it was the blatant disrespect I received from my parents and my parents-in-law that assured me that my son would be living in a cesspool of emotional abuse if he went into their care. I felt then, as I do now, that his best chances were with me. I wouldn't even consider outside adoption, either, so I did my best to provide structure as I was learning it. I didn't think it was the worst thing in the world to continue raising my child as I got well. Indeed, it was my intention to provide a stable, loving home for him.

Matthew was turning five by the time, with Mary's help, I finally faced my alcoholism. One of my biggest fears when considering sobriety was, *What am I going to do with all the free time I spent drinking?* The hardest time for me to get through was from 3 p.m., when I got home from work, until 5 p.m., when I could busy myself preparing supper. (Yes, I did most of my drinking at home.) That fear was quashed when I began almost daily walks with Matthew to the ice-cream shop. Before that time, I didn't have a sweet tooth, as I kept my sugar needs well supplied with beer, but, boy, did I crave the sweets when I stopped drinking beer. Besides eating ice cream, I also baked chocolate cakes and drank lots of sweet grape soda. I didn't gain any weight from all these added sweets, though. The activities I added evened things out for me. On snowy nights, for example, I got out the sled and pulled Matthew all around town. It was so beautiful! Our sled rides became a nightly event because the world was just so much prettier at night and there wasn't as much traffic to contend with. Sometimes we went to the grocery store, and he'd hold the groceries in his lap as I pulled the sled home. These times I spent with Matthew are some of my happier memories. As he got older, we cross-country skied, and when the season changed, we went swimming and rode bikes together.

The fact that I had to learn to become playful in recovery allowed Matthew and me to have some pretty decent quality time together. There were times, of course, when I didn't think he wanted to have fun, and I soon began suspecting he was getting his kicks out of trying to wreck my fun. I was struggling with being a good mother. What was I doing wrong? Why wasn't he responding to the changes I've been making to stabilize his life? I felt guilty about having to work, but it was a necessity. Other than work and attending my two AA meetings a week, I was home with him all the time. Although my original contract to work with an alcoholism counselor had long expired, I still went to sessions with counselors from time to time. I needed continuing guidance and, more importantly, the assurance that I was offering Matthew the guidance he needed in his life.

Mary, by the way, was correct in suggesting that Matthew might perhaps do better if placed in a different home. While she had no more knowledge about ADD than I did, she assumed correctly that Matthew and I would need more guidance than she was capable of offering. Matthew was so young, yet he was displaying the anger often associated with children who grow up in alcoholic homes. Although he didn't strike out or hit, he was angry and distrustful when interacting with anyone, and he had passive-aggressive behaviors. There were many days when my only source of comfort and strength was my belief that God believed I would be the best mother for Matthew, and on those days I had to keep reminding myself of this. There were other days when I wondered if God had a sense of humor and was having himself a good laugh watching me struggle with such an opposing personality as my son.

Even though we lived in the same small town, Stan had almost no presence in Matthew's life. About the time Matthew turned eight, I accepted the fact that I wasn't going to be able to encourage a father-son relationship.

My intuition began encouraging me to move to a more populated part of our state, and I found another nurse's aide job at another nursing home. One thing was certain: there seemed to always be a shortage of nurse's aides at the time, and it was fairly easy for me to get a job. Nursing aide jobs were easy to come by, but desirable shifts were another matter. I had to work evenings for the first six months before I could get a coveted day shift. Regardless of what shift an aide works, they are going to be working at least every other weekend, too. After we moved, it was very difficult for Matthew, having strangers for babysitters in a strange city where we didn't know anybody. I make friends easily, and moving was an exciting adventure for me, but I didn't consider my son's opposite personality or how difficult it might be for him to make friends or adjust to moving. It wasn't long after our move before I was seeking help for Matthew with a family therapist.

After living in our new city for perhaps a year, I became aware of a treatment center there that had an AODA counselor training program. This was a one-year program with coursework followed by an apprenticeship, working for that year in the treatment center. This training program is where I became good friends with Jackie, who also had a previous career of being a nurse's aide. She and I laughed and said our priorities for becoming trainees were finding jobs where we could carry clipboards and drink coffee while we worked. Actually, as we were both single mothers, we wanted day jobs that didn't require working weekends and evenings.

The training program was intense, and the recruiters were less than honest as to actual hours spent at the center. Between taking classes, learning the administrative responsibilities required of the job, and then putting in the apprenticeship hours, I was required to be away from home up to seventy hours per week. Oh, yes—apprenticeship also meant working all shifts and holidays. It was a year of Jackie and me whining that we were trying to do the right thing for our children, and here we were, bringing our jammies to work. During this time, one of my sisters came to live with us to be there for Matthew and try to make his home life as normal as possible. It was during times when my sister needed to be elsewhere and I called a babysitter that Matthew rebelled at having me gone so much. He started stealing from stores. This is when we ended up seeing a court-appointed family therapist.

As Matthew's passive-aggressive behaviors, defiance of me, and school participation were all becoming worse and worse, I became aware of available help (thanks to the apprenticeship program) and arranged for him to be placed in a group home where he'd receive the help I believed he needed. Although Stan had been absent from Matthew's life for all these years, the court-appointed therapist felt he should be included in making the group home placement decision. My intuition was screaming not to call Stan, but I went against my gut feeling and I called him. When I told Stan the situation, his Higher Power—his mother—insisted that Matthew come live with them until I completed my training program six months later. So instead of getting any help, when Matthew was ten years old, he went to live with his father's family. No matter how distraught I was though, one thing I didn't have to worry about was that progress he had made would be lost while he was there. There had never been any progress made! I worried about his being emotionally abused while living with Stan's parents.

No matter how much I tried to provide stability for Matthew from the time he was very small, he remained distrustful of me. He was unforgiving. He always acted as if he were ashamed of me and angry at me. I could never make any progress with him. He was so good at blocking all nurturing that I never felt like we had a loving mother-son relationship. I was always looking for a glimmer of light, something to show that he had broken through his cloud of darkness and distrust and we would finally be able to live comfortably together. Except for my sister, who was living with Matthew and me, my family and Stan's blamed me for Matthew's misery and behavior problems. I never trusted what either family told him about me. I was always sure they were filling his head with stories that kept him confused and unsure of me. His behavior was just so unusual that I now think we were all pointing fingers, trying to make sense of it. But nothing ever made any sense. Because I was his primary caregiver, it made perfect sense to everyone, even to me, that I was the one to blame for his unhappiness. It was something I did, something I said. Something! I kept hoping that someday I'd figure it out, and my son would be able to feel happiness.

One day after he returned home and living with me again, Matthew told me one of his grandmother's accusations. I had completed my AODA training and was working as a counselor, but was home from work on a sick day. He told me he didn't think I was really sick, that I wasn't really working. He said Grandma had told him that if his mother had ever worked a day in her life, she'd spin in her grave. She'd told him that when I said I was going to work, I was actually going out to spend my days with men. This is the same woman who, during the few years I was married to her son, scolded me all the time for working too hard! I will never understand how anyone could deliberately hurt a child in such a way.

Matthew's temporary placement with his grandmother, regardless of what she may or may not have told him didn't seem to make any difference in his life. I couldn't see where he might have regressed, but neither did I see any improvements. Matthew remained Matthew. A friend who frequently observed us interacting said, "He won't let you nurture him!" At least I had someone validating that empty hole in me where my motherly love and pride should have been. I was several years sober by now, after years of therapy, and I was working as an AODA counselor. I was still attending both AA and Al-Anon meetings, too. I had begun attending Al-Anon meetings during my counselor training program because the disharmony in our home was so stressful for me. The meetings proved to be very beneficial. It was there that I began accepting the fact that I couldn't change Matthew. He was the only one who could make those changes, and only if he wanted to. As a therapist, I guided and encouraged families to make the same changes I made early in my recovery. I watched them develop healthy, loving, forgiving relationships.

I hadn't been working at this AODA counseling agency for long, however, when they closed their doors. I was out of a job. Now what was I going to do? Matthew was asking that we move back north so he would be nearer his dad. He wanted a relationship with Stan and felt that would happen if we lived nearer, but I liked where we were living. I made so many wonderful friendships and really didn't want to leave. So I considered the pros and cons of moving. Job security in the AODA field would be greatly reduced by a move north. Matthew had seen little of his father while living at Grandma's, and I was pretty sure a move wasn't going to change anything. Ultimately, I acknowledged that my move to the city had been a selfish act and probably not the best thing I could have done for Matthew, so with a heavy heart, I moved back to the northern region of our state and limited my job search to that area. Now Matthew could live near his dad. I also set him up with his own therapist for weekly sessions.

From the beginning of my recovery, I encouraged Matthew to talk to me, to my therapists, and eventually to his own therapist. But for his weekly one-hour visit, he sat in the therapist's office and refused to say a word. He told me that nobody was going to pick his brain. He often heard from others that his mother was such a nice lady, but he always thought, *Yeah, well, you don't live with her.* Matthew had contact with a variety of mental health professionals as a child, and he was always considered to be a rebellious, passive-aggressive, difficult child. No one thought he might be suffering a disability. None of the professionals discussed the possibility with me that perhaps Matthew suffered from a mental condition, or that he might have confusion in his thought process that could possibly be corrected with medication. Medication for him was never discussed.

"Children aren't stupid," I was told by more than one professional. "If you're feeling all the pain and hurt for him when he does poorly, why should he bother with it? You're doing it all for him, and that puts a kid in a very powerful position. He can screw up all he wants. He's not suffering the consequences for his screwups. That's how he will keep punishing you." This is good advice to parents of children *without* disabilities, but not good advice for me in my situation. I conducted my parenting of Matthew believing that some day there would be a breakthrough, that someday he would forgive me.

After moving back to our hometown, I was able to secure a part-time "woman's consultant" position in the AODA field, but that was only after I put in many volunteer hours at the outpatient agency to prove my abilities. Money was very tight until my part-time position finally developed into a full-time position.

Next, Mathew refused to go to school. I sent him off to school each day and left for work, but he hid in the toolshed instead of getting on the bus. After I was out of sight, he came out and spent a comfortable day at home with the heat jacked up to 85 degrees. I sometimes drove him to school and watched him walk in; as I drove off, he walked out the back doors of the school.

By the time Matthew was fourteen, he was so rebellious that professionals working with us thought foster home placement might benefit him. They felt that if he learned that all homes have rules and expectations, he would be more compliant with me. When Matthew left home for foster care placement, I cried for two weeks. Though I knew it was supposed to be short-term placement, I also knew in my heart he would never really be back home. Most parents don't do their empty nest grieving until their children reach eighteen and leave for college; I did my grieving when my son was only fourteen.

Matthew's foster parent was a young, single man who had his heart in the right place. He owned his own home and wanted to share what he had with foster sons. It seemed to me that he had to make some mighty big adjustments in his personal life to become an overnight parent to adolescents with behavior problems, but he felt he could offer male guidance and improve the boys' lives. Matthew was this young man's first foster son. It was decided that foster care wasn't the answer, and Matthew came home after six months. After this one trial placement, the young man decided he probably wasn't the most qualified to teach Matthew social appropriateness. Later, I unexpectedly ran into the man, and he seemed happy to have an opportunity to ask me about something that had been bothering him. One day he and Matthew had been wrestling, and he thought they were having a good time, rolling around on the floor and laughing. All of a sudden, Matthew coughed up some mucus and, "He spit that stuff right on top of my head! Why did he do that? We were having fun, and he did that to me!" That poor man couldn't understand, and I had little help to offer. I always thought that Matthew's refusal to allow me to nurture him was similar to my childhood attempts to protect myself, and I explained to the former foster parent that I thought Matthew might have actually found himself liking him and was enjoying himself, and it scared him. I thought he had reacted by doing something repulsive that it would keep the foster parent guarded and wary of future attempts at bonding.

Besides being unable to convince this young man to go another round with Matthew, Social Services wasn't able to convince any other foster parents to take on Matthew's behaviors and problems, either. Eventually, due to his habitual truancy, a judge felt Matthew needed encouragement to understand that children were required to go to school and to live by the rules of society. First, the judge requested a mental health evaluation for appropriate placement. Would he be placed in a juvenile detention center or a facility that focused more effectively with mental health issues?

I was finally going to get some real help! Because I was working in the AODA field, I was getting information on ADD—what to look for and how to make a referral for a mental health evaluation if I suspected any of my clients might be suffering this disability. I knew Matthew fit all the criteria for ADD, but so far he had not been professionally diagnosed. Now he was going into a lockup ward in a hospital for a two-week evaluation. The clinic at this hospital was diagnosing many small children with ADD and sending them home with prescriptions for Ritalin. I thought how exciting it would be for those at the clinic to work with an older version of an untreated child with ADD. I thought they could learn from working with Matthew.

But the clinic determined that Matthew was a troubled juvenile who would benefit from lockup. Off to jail my son went. He was sixteen years old. The judge told him it could be for just six months. Or it could be longer. It depended on when he was ready to go to school and follow society's rules.

Three different men, acquaintances who worked at the paper mill in town, called me. All three said basically the same thing, "My son [or nephew] just got back from a hospital where he went for an evaluation and was diagnosed with ADD. I'm looking through the brochures, and, well, I couldn't help but think of you. I remember all the problems you had with your son. Did you know your son has ADD?"

Having three common laborers who could accurately diagnose what the professionals could not threw sand into my open wounds. I was enormously angry that the clinic had said my son needed to be jailed. All my professional peers told me to let it go, to not fight it. My son was so incredibly obnoxious and antisocial that most people who knew me were glad I was getting a break from him … even if it meant inappropriate lockup.

And it's true. Although I was angry about the clinic's missed diagnosis, I didn't grieve as much when Matthew was placed in juvenile lockup, as I did when he left for foster care. I was furious with God, and my fury burned faster than any slow, smoldering anger. How could God have let my son slip through the cracks? I finally had an answer that helped explain Matthew's behavior. But it was useless. It was too little, too late. After all those years, regardless how hard I tried, cried, and prayed, it was never God's will that I help my son. I had to expand my limited realm of thinking and beliefs to accept my son's unhappiness as something I could not change. Matthew's circumstances certainly gave credibility to the idea of destiny: that before he was born, he agreed to these difficulties in life and that *he* would be the only one who could make those changes in his life. Knowing he was in a safe place now, I decided not to worry about what he was or wasn't doing. I was better able to begin letting him go. He was the one who needed to come to terms with himself … if he was going to. He was out of my hands. I thought I'd let him worry about himself while I just enjoyed life for a while.

I began to relax. I enjoyed my hours of peaceful solitude after a day's work. I relaxed in hot baths. While relaxing in the wonderful warmth, I bellowed out to the Nothingness, "Does it bother you that I'm relaxing in the tub and you can't disturb me?" Although by this time I had been sober for eleven years, I was still attending an Al-Anon and AA meeting each week. This is a lot of meetings for someone with that many years of sobriety, but I needed to sustain my sanity and serenity. I knew Matthew was a constant source of stress for me, and within two months of his departure I truly came to realize what an enormous emotional disruption he had been. I was able to maintain my composure while attending significantly fewer meetings.

Up to now, it seemed that my life consisted of my recovery from alcoholism and undoing the damage of being raised in a dysfunctional home. I had struggled to provide stability for my son. Despite having times when I felt God was testing my will, I never lost the gratitude for my recovery I felt the time I imitated Richard Nixon at a meeting. Early in recovery, I made an enormous mistake in getting involved with a male AA member who was not sincere about recovery. After that, I dated a few times but never considered anyone to be much more than just an evening out. Matthew was determined to keep men out of my life. Whenever I had a date, he displayed his most obnoxious behavior, knowing they wouldn't stick around long.

While Matthew was living with his foster parent, I began spending evenings out with friends. I became involved in activities I previously hadn't found time for. I joined a swimming class and women's volleyball team. After an evening of volleyball, I asked my friend Ginger to stop at a gas station convenience store to check out a guy who worked there. I had stopped by earlier, and the assistant manager began flirting outrageously with me. I didn't know who he was, but he acted like he knew me. I didn't trust my intuition in the men department and wanted a second opinion.

"*Eeuuwweeee!*" Ginger laughed when we got back into the car. "He likes you! He wants to take you to bed!"

"But didn't you see he's wearing a class ring on his wedding-band finger?" I asked. "Major red flag! He's just divorced, and I don't want to deal with someone just out of a relationship."

"Oh, go for it," she said.

The next time I stopped in, he asked me for a date. I accepted. That first date was the start of the rest of my life with Benjamin.

Benjamin knew who I was. Some of his friends had advised him that we had a lot in common and encouraged him to ask me out. His friends were right. We were compatible. We clicked. We hadn't dated for long when he said those three magic words: "I'll cook tonight." I knew he was a keeper.

During the first two years, we had a few bumps in the relationship. Benjamin, who was childless, had a lot to consider in getting involved with someone who had a minor son, and such a rebellious one. He certainly didn't want to be straddled with a woman who would forever be trying to make a man out of a son who clearly didn't want any responsibilities. During these two years, my son was first in foster care, then living wherever he had the least expectations on placed him, sometimes with me, other times with his dad; usually in a friend's car. When he went to juvenile lockup, it was for an undetermined period of time. When he was ready to attend school, that's when he'd be discharged.

Benjamin was indeed newly divorced. He had some lingering issues and unfairly lumped all women into one category. As far as I was concerned, he was lacking in the respect department, too. He seemed to have left his marriage determined to never marry again, or, for that matter, never be exclusively involved with one woman. The man just never had it in him to be a womanizer. He might have had grandiose wishes, but he lacked the temperament for it. And he was going to do what he wanted to do, darn it all! He let me know that he watched football on weekends, and I was not to expect him to do anything else. Looking back, I suppose he was a little suspicious of my behavior, but I was quite content to curl up with a good novel while he watched the games. This was the quiet, at-home life I had been longing for. I know it takes years to work through the hurt of a divorce, so I was patient and gave him time to sort things through and figure out I was deserving of more respect than he was willing to give.

It didn't look to me like Matthew's time in lockup would be only six months. It looked like he was hell-bent on showing all of us that he did not have to attend school. He quickly learned that attending classes was considered a privilege in lockup, so he remained just disruptive enough that he was confined to a cottage where all privileges were restricted. It was here that he had the least human contact and minimal expectations were placed on him. He seemed comfortable there. He wasn't motivated to work toward discharge. He was waiting until he turned eighteen, when he would be discharged simply for outgrowing juvenile status.

So my son was gone, and my relationship with Benjamin was looking more and more like it was headed for a dead end. As much as I was able to see his positive attributes, I had already given him two years to understand I didn't belong in his little category of "all women." I had fallen hard for this guy, but I was not going to compromise myself or accept disrespectful behavior. I wasn't willing to wait and hope that he would begin treating me with more respect. I also knew it would be very difficult for me to live in the same small town as him and eventually have him start dating someone else. Nothing was holding me in my hometown anymore. I was free to return to the city where I had enjoyed living before and still had friends.

There were several positions in the AODA field available in the city, and when I sought another counseling position, I was happy to be hired at the first agency I applied to. I was able to reestablish old friendships. Five months later, while I was settling into my new life, my intuition told me to call Benjamin. I resisted for a couple of hours, thinking, *I wouldn't know what to say. I don't have anything that I want to say to him.* Finally, my intuition said, *Don't worry about what to say. The words will come.*

Benjamin was glad to get my call. He had been trying to find me. First, he asked if he could come for a visit, then, he said he was going back home to sell his house and belongings and would be right back to start over with me. He said he wanted "to do it right this time."

"Uh, wait a minute," I said. "This is moving too fast for me." But I was standing in his cloud of dust as he hightailed it for home. He was able to sell his home and most of his belongings with amazing speed, and within a month he was able to fit his remaining earthly possessions into his conversion van and move in with me. Our reunion worked. I'll admit that this time I was the one not entirely trusting the changes Benjamin seemed to have made, but his changes were for real, and I have thanked myself many times for listening to my guides when they encouraged me to call him that night.

About this time, Benjamin was offered a job as a utility pole safety inspector for a company based out of Buffalo, New York. He would be foreman of a small crew inspecting utility poles throughout the United States. Benjamin is an adventurous man, and the thought of traveling so much and staying in each location only a month or two was appealing to him. He was also going to be making an excellent wage in the process. But he said he wouldn't even consider the position if I didn't join him. I could work as a crew member.

After all the training I had put in to become an AODA counselor and five years of work gaining experience and credibility in the field, I had finally secured a position that was fully compensating me for my efforts. I was not, therefore, eager to give up this coveted position if Benjamin's job was only short-term. I also didn't know if I had the flexibility to leave the state and live elsewhere while my minor son was in lockup. After contacting his social worker and discussing the situation I was contemplating, I was told there was no reason for me to have to stay in the state.

So Benjamin and I compromised. He would spend two months in Indiana, training for the job and deciding if he really wanted to stay with the company. I would continue working where I was. Once he decided to stay with the job, I gave my two weeks' notice. While he waited for me to join him, he bought an eighteen-foot travel trailer, which could be hitched to his truck, for us to live in. When I made the move to Indiana it was without any hesitation. I was comfortable with my decision to step out of the counseling field and into the great outdoors and didn't question if I was doing the right thing. This move came a few months before Christmas. I began work with Benjamin as his crew member. For the first time in my life, I was not working directly with people.

When Benjamin and I joined households, even though we had both sold most of our possessions, we found we still had too much stuff. As Christmas approached, we found a church that accepted material donations and forwarded our truckload of almost new household furnishings and items to families in the Appalachian Mountains. Benjamin and I both felt that was the best Christmas we ever had. It gave us a sense of what we felt Christmas should be.

Safety inspection of utility poles is physically hard work. It kept us in shape, and by the time we walked the lines that needed inspection, we often knew streets and towns better than most people who lived there. One summer, we started on a line in Illinois, right across the river from Missouri. The line took us to the middle of Illinois. The next summer, when we picked up where we'd left off, we ended twenty miles short of the Indiana border. We had literally walked across the state of Illinois. We saw many beautiful sights, too. I once came upon the birthing of a calf as I walked through a pasture. I watched that little fellow stand up and take his first steps.

One day in Georgia, as I was putting my work equipment into the truck at the end of the day, I smelled the most wonderful aromas coming from a home nearby. I could hear something frying in a pan, and the smells were tantalizing. The house was what most of us would recognize as a tool shed, a very dilapidated tool shed. Both sides were braced up with two-by-fours, and the roofing was held in place by concrete blocks on the corners. Just as I realized that this tool shed was actually a home, I saw the most beautiful black woman come outside to relax and catch some of the cool, late afternoon breeze. She had her hair tied up under a white kerchief and wore a stiffly ironed white blouse and a long white skirt. She looked so proud, so serene, so dignified. She dusted something from her shoulder, then sat on her front step to enjoy the cool afternoon.

When Benjamin came to the truck, I told him he had to get a picture of the woman sitting on her step. "She is the most beautiful woman I've ever seen," I told him. As we drove by, he took her picture, and because it was a noisy self-winding camera, she looked over at us. She was angry that we had taken a picture of her. I felt so guilty for invading her privacy that it took me eleven years before I could enlarge the picture. From the time I asked Benjamin to take the picture, I had intended to enlarge it to an eight-by-ten print and frame it. Now I keep her picture in the bathroom, where I see her every day while I brush my teeth and comb my hair. It's a perfect reminder of the lesson, "Lord, keep me humble."

Benjamin and I soon upgraded to a thirty-five-foot travel trailer, which we also pulled behind his work truck. On weekends, we took our tent and went exploring where our job didn't take us. Benjamin is full of adventure, so we always had something fun to do. Wherever we went, he hired a small work crew, so when Matthew turned eighteen and was released, Benjamin hired him to work with us. We let him use our tent and got permission from the campground owners for him to set it up on our site. Our hope was that he would realize how fortunate he was to get a better than minimum-wage-paying job without the benefit of much more than a grade-school education. We encouraged him to save money so that he had a nest egg to fall back on or to be able to purchase a car in the future.

After Matthew had been working with us for only eight months, however, Benjamin had to fire him. He was never ready for work when he told him to be. Every morning, we had to wake him up and wait for him. We showed him several times how to plan and prepare lunches for himself, but at lunchtime we found that he either had not fixed a lunch or didn't have money to buy anything. Whether it was because he was hungry, or something else, his work

31

was unsatisfactory. Benjamin and I had to buy a bus ticket for him to go from Georgia to relatives in our northern state. We hoped that he would be more responsible on his next job.

Working with Benjamin was fun for me. Workdays were often like play days. Being outside and exploring places we'd never been was an adventure, and we got paid to do it! Although the crewmembers were paid above minimum wage, however, I was used to bigger paychecks than I was getting, and the work was very strenuous. I decided that if I was going to work that hard, I was going to train to be a foreman and get paid what I felt was a decent wage. The company promised that after I finished my training, they would place us on contracted jobs that required more than one foreman and crew. Benjamin worked a contract in Danville, Illinois, while I went to Moline for my training. Now I was alone in the conversion van and the tent. I camped for a month in a campground on the Mississippi River while I trained for the foreman position.

Benjamin and I had been inspecting utility poles for almost four years when he said, "Well, that was fun. Now what do you want to do?" He thought we should make a tour of the western part of the United States because we hadn't traveled there as part of our job. He also thought we should stop off in Las Vegas and get married. He told me that I "passed all the tests with flying colors." We got married in Las Vegas in 1992, then drove to San Diego, where I had relatives and friends, whom we visited for a few days. From there, we drove the coastal route to Washington state, where Benjamin had lived when he was a young man and just discharged from the army. We traveled in a newer conversion van and still had our tent, so our journey was a long camping trip. It was great. One purpose of the trip was trying to figure out where we wanted to live. Washington was good, and his old job was there if he wanted it back. But we also liked South Carolina. We had lived there for awhile, and it was hard for me not to go back, but we finally decided to return to our home state. His mother and stepfather still lived there, and when he was working on the road, Benjamin missed family during the holidays.

We bought ten peaceful rural acres and continued living in our travel trailer while we built the lower level of our home. We built a small cottage, much like ones Benjamin had seen while he was stationed in Germany. He loved the small country cottages with flower gardens surrounding them. He let me go wild with flowers. Well, at first he was cautious. He was afraid they wouldn't grow, and he didn't want me to be disappointed, but I assured him that if they didn't grow, I'd keep planting more until they did. We gave ourselves five years to build the home, complete with garage. We built as we had money and did the work ourselves. This way we avoided having a mortgage.

My adventurous outdoor man got himself a job at the local paper mill. "I can do anything for five years," he said. He worked swing shifts at the mill, which led to a continuous rotation of sleeping hours. When he was on the night shift, he had a difficult time sleeping during the day and developed a very ugly mood. Soon I was thinking, *I married this man, and now I'm not so sure I like him very much.*

Benjamin had been working at the mill for about a year, when I walked upstairs one day and heard him talking to someone on the telephone. He was calling a truck driving school and asking if there were any openings. Almost in tears, he said, "I'm working at the paper mill now, and *they don't have any windows!*" That poor man! I understood perfectly. There was no way I could work somewhere and not be able to at least look outside. So off he went to learn to drive over-the-road semitrailer trucks.

By now, we were financially stable enough that I didn't need to go back to work. I continued to work on the house, doing most of the home maintenance and yard work, things I loved doing. I also picked up frequent short-term jobs. We live near potato fields, and I enjoy farming, so every spring I planted potatoes and every fall I harvested them. I also worked at a nearby vitamin wholesale shop when the owner got large orders and needed extra help. Then I started teaching Group Dynamics classes and the Multiple Offender Program at our area technical school. These are programs that offenders of "operating while impaired" laws are required to take after they have been assessed as not having a drinking problem; Group Dynamics for first-time offenders and Multiple Offender Program for two or more arrests. Offenders who are assessed as having a problematic drinking pattern are referred for counseling, just as I had been. I never talked about my having been arrested in my classes, as I felt it would distract students into thinking, *Just because she got arrested and quit drinking, she wants everyone to quit.* I could effectively provide the information required in an educational setting and allow each student to make his or her own decisions regarding drinking. All of these part-time jobs were flexible and gave me free time to ride with Benjamin when we wanted to be together.

I enjoyed traveling with Benjamin. Riding in the semis with him was always fun, so I went with him fairly often. Sometimes we put all three of our dogs in the semi with us, while other times we hired dog sitters. We had Scooby, a Brittany spaniel, and Missy and Prince Albert, Springer spaniels. When I traveled with Benjamin, he tried getting loads headed to fun spots like Florida, where we could take time to swim in the ocean. Sometimes, we unhooked the trailer and went sightseeing in the truck. Driving across the bayous of New Orleans in a semi offers sightseeing vistas not available in smaller vehicles. We didn't think life could get much better.

We often laughed about the life we were leading. Benjamin had thought he'd love to drive semi, but it wouldn't be a good job for him if he was married. I had imagined myself living alone in a small cottage with flower and vegetable gardens. It took us coming together for our dreams to materialize, and we had a happy, loving marriage besides. The day we married, I told Benjamin, "You've just embarked on the greatest adventure of your life." Our life together has been adventurous, but in ways we never expected. God had some surprises ready for us. Our strong commitment to each other pulled us through a most difficult challenge and made our relationship stronger.

# Chapter 3

## *Steven Enters Our Lives*

Shortly after his return home from Georgia, Matthew moved to a small city an hour's drive from our hometown. His father had moved there, and Matthew was still hopeful that they would have a better relationship. It was there that he met Tina. Having raised Matthew in an alcohol-free environment, at least for the most part, I questioned his attraction to her, but although he never married Tina, he remained in a relationship with her for ten years. That relationship produced my awesome grandson, Steven, the dear young man who asked me to write his story.

I first met Tina when she was seventeen (a year younger than Matthew), and it was obvious to me right away that she was already suffering emotional problems that needed treatment. Tina had serious problems with alcohol and drug addiction arising, I was certain, from a miserable, tragic childhood. I also suspected that she was anorexic. She told me her mother was an alcoholic and, though committed for treatment several times, never remained sober. She said that she and her brother lived periodically with their grandmother, then later in a foster home. I could see Tina needed love and understanding, but these had to be on her terms, and her terms did not include her making any efforts to compromise or change. Matthew and Tina were two troubled young adults who found companionship and comfort with each other, but I knew the disease and insanity of alcoholism well enough to be sure that the comfort my son provided Tina would not sustain her for long.

When I interacted with Tina in the early days of their relationship, I couldn't help but think, *There but for the grace of God go I*. Tina was so immature that talking to her was like talking to a child. I couldn't help but wonder if that was how I had seemed before my therapy. I found myself giving her the same *that's okay* hand gestures I used to get, and I heard myself telling her, "That's okay. You don't have to explain." My God! That *was* me before therapy! Was Matthew comfortable around her because she reminded him of his childhood? He was having enough problems managing his own life, and I couldn't help but wonder how long it would take him to understand he was in over his head with another life complicated with drugs and alcohol. As a child and adolescent, he had often questioned me about my parents' or siblings' drunken behaviors, which he found offensive. I knew he must have understood that choosing a life with Tina would lead to a life full of chaos. Of course he could also choose a less complicated life, one free from drugs and alcohol. I wished he would make such a choice.

Matthew and Tina lived together for about a year when she began insisting that they have a baby. She even brought the subject up in my presence a few times, hoping, of course, that I would encourage Matthew to make me a grandmother. "Babies are so cute," she'd coo. "I want to put his little backpack on him and watch him walk off for his first day at school." Matthew would explode with, "How can we take care of a baby? We can't even take care of ourselves!" Hearing his reaction always assured me that he was in touch with reality and would be cautious, knowing they were ill-equipped for parenthood. But Tina progressed to obsessively pressuring him, and I became fearful that she just might get what she wanted. Because she wasn't getting pregnant fast enough, she even went so far as to check into fertility treatments. She had a state-funded medical card, she reasoned, so it wouldn't cost them anything.

Tina is a master manipulator. About a year later they visited Benjamin and me to tell us the good news that we were to be grandparents. Matthew seemed genuinely hurt that we didn't squeal in delight. We didn't say (or indicate in any way), "Oh, how could you?" We just weren't able to express much happiness. Truthfully, Benjamin and I were devastated. Our hearts went out to this unborn child. What kind of a chance would it have?

"I thought you wanted to be a grandma," my son said.

"I've always told you there was no rush to make me a grandma," I replied. "I could wait." As I write this, I still wonder how he interpreted my feelings as encouragement to produce a baby. Whatever happened to his understanding that they weren't stable enough in their own lives to become parents?

They continued living near Stan, and although it was an hour and a half drive, I made several trips during the pregnancy and tried to stay supportive and involved. Matthew was getting excited about becoming a father, but he asked me not to tell my family his good news. "All they'll say," he told me, "is 'How does he expect to take care of a baby when he can't take care of himself?'" Parenthood was going to be difficult enough without the added negative energy of their comments. I believe negative thoughts are harmful, and I was amazed at what I saw as his brilliance in believing negativity is harmful, even if we don't hear the negative comments. There's a fine line between negativity and reality sometimes; if the truth hurts, and you are hearing the same thing from several different people, perhaps there is something going on that you need to consider changing.

During Tina's pregnancy, they were living in a studio apartment and sharing a bathroom with other renters. When I made my second or third visit to the expectant parents' apartment, Tina's mother was there. This was my introduction to Julie, or Meme. "You can be Grandma," she told me, "and I'll be Meme. After all, it's my daughter who's having the baby!" Meme certainly seemed excited about her impending grandmotherhood. I considered putting my worries aside. Maybe Tina would receive guidance from her mother, and the baby would be properly cared for. But Meme's big hair (a wig) distracted me. It was only 8:30 in the morning, and the style of the wig was much too elaborate for the casual slacks and blouse she was wearing; besides, it was sitting slightly askew. Her nose was flat and crooked, the result of having been broken a few times, and if she wore dentures, she hadn't slipped them in yet, though she didn't appear to be missing them. When I remembered Tina's stories about her and her brother being placed in foster care, my worries actually deepened. I understood that Meme would probably have great influence with Tina's decisions.

Matthew and Tina had already picked up a used crib. The morning I first met Meme, I arrived early enough that they were all just getting up. Meme was using the crib mattress on the floor as her bed. After a few more visits, I saw clearly that Meme was living with Matthew and Tina. Regardless of the time I arrived, things weren't put away, and it was obvious that the crib mattress was her bed.

Steven was born July 18, 1996. Thanks to his mother's "failure to progress" to regular delivery, he arrived by Cesarean section. When he was three days old, he was admitted to intensive care for cardiac evaluation because he was having periods of rapid heartbeat. This condition was monitored and treated with Popranolol for his first nine months of life, but he had only a few episodes those first few days and has had no further complications.

I met Steven when he was ten days old, after he had been released from the hospital. He was a beautiful little boy who was sleeping when I first saw him. I was able to feed him a bottle of milk that first visit, and some of his behavior made me suspect from the start that there might be autistic complications. That may sound like a grandiose diagnosis, but let me explain. All the while I fed him from his bottle, he ever so gently rubbed the tips of his fingers over the knuckles of my hand, which was holding the bottle. He rubbed my knuckles continuously, and the rubbing made my skin tender. I checked his fingertips for redness or obvious indications that his tender newborn skin was getting irritated, but I could see no evidence of this. When I tried holding his hand to stop the rubbing, he became irritable, and even at just ten days old, he was able to disengage my hand and resume rubbing my knuckles, frantically at first, then calming down only after he satisfied himself with the sensations he was seeking. How did I recognize autistic behavior in a newborn baby? I really can't say for sure, other than I must have read something on autism and repetitive behaviors, and I thought it was telling how he became so frantic when I disrupted the rubbing. That was not normal newborn behavior, and my intuition was kicking in, big-time. I kept my mouth shut, though. There was no need to upset the new family with what might be a needless fear.

After my initial visit, I made plans for additional visits and made the three-hour round-trips only to find no one home. I called many times asking for a convenient time for them to have me visit. I asked that I could bring my friend Jackie from the AODA counselor training program with me for what became my seventh trip to visit my grandson, only to have him not home again.

During her pregnancy, Tina had told me about how she and her brother had been pawns in the game Meme played with their father. She didn't allow the children to visit him. When they rode their bikes to their father's house, Meme called the police to bring them home. It wasn't that her father was a bad man, Tina explained. Meme just liked to play these types of games. So I knew who was behind the disappearing acts at my prearranged visits.

During my seventh visit, therefore, Tina was home, but Aunt Violet and Meme had taken Steven to a church service. This was on a Thursday afternoon. "I will not be calling or asking if I can arrange a visit anymore," I told Tina. "I am simply going to come. And I am not going to knock on your door. I am simply going to walk in. Do you understand why I will no longer be trying to prearrange visits?" She nodded her head, and I never again made the trip without seeing my grandson. I seldom made a trip after the tenth of any month, however. Both Tina and Meme received Supplemental Security Income from Social Security, and although my son worked, they were always broke by the tenth of the month. If I visited any later in the month, they asked me to buy them things.

Before going to school to become an AODA counselor, I had worked several years as a nurse's aide and witnessed both petite and grand mal seizures. During a visit in November 1996, when Steven was four months old, I noticed he was having what I knew to be petite seizures. Knowing that Tina was emotionally and mentally fragile, I showed her what he was doing and asked if she had ever noticed. "Yeah," she said. "Sometimes he makes really stupid faces."

I explained as carefully as I could that the "really stupid faces" might be a very serious medical condition and that he needed to see a doctor as soon as possible. Breaking my own rule, I made another trip later that month to see if she had followed through and made a doctor's appointment. She said she had, but the doctor said it was only colic. During my visit, I noticed Steven having another petite seizure. I pointed it out and told Tina that she had to get him back to the doctor.

I visited again the first of the next month. Tina had taken Steven back to the doctor, and again the doctor had said he had colic. It was during this visit that I first heard Tina suggest to Matthew that they should give Steven to Social Services. That's what she said—that they should just "give him up." She had this discussion with Matthew in my presence, so I knew she no longer wanted the responsibility of a baby. I am sure she assumed that I would jump up and demand to raise him. So much for her wonderful visions of having an adorable little boy to send off to school wearing his little backpack. It was obvious that they'd had this discussion before and were bringing it up now for my benefit. Matthew bellowed, "You don't give your kids away! You raise them yourself!"

That day, I went home and wrote my first letter to the Social Services Department. I didn't know that Social Services were already trying to be involved in protecting Steven. I stated that I hoped they were aware of a family in need of guidance and that I suspected that at some point the baby would be in need of temporary foster care. Should that time come, I added, I wanted to be considered for the responsibility of caring for Steven.

Benjamin, who was on the road, called home every evening. That evening, when I told him about my letter to Social Services, we had our first big argument. He flatly refused to take responsibility for Tina's irresponsible behavior. Before we married, Benjamin and I had discussed whether or not we wanted to raise children. We were still young enough that had we wanted children, and we could have had our own family, but we agreed that raising children was not what we wanted to do. Benjamin was angry and hurt that I had volunteered to care for Steven without first discussing it with him. This responsibility could begin the next day if Tina knew I had made myself available. I think she would have gladly dumped the kid, and Benjamin was

39

afraid that was just what she would do. He is also adamant that each person has to be responsible for their own behavior and choices.

When I talked about our big fight with a couple of friends, I was more in the position of defending Benjamin than arguing for my point of view. I understood his position. I felt the same way. I understood how he was angry that I had made such a decision without discussing it with him. But I saw only a need for protecting that baby. I assumed my husband would understand and support me. I was appalled that he seemed to take the position that we wouldn't do anything to help Steven. The situation was gut-wrenching for me, but I knew Social Services had already been contacted. I suspected that when the time came for foster care, I'd have to admit to Social Services that I would not be able to take on the responsibility, after all. Thanks to years of therapy, I am one of those people who can actually accept no as an answer. I don't hope, pray, or try to manipulate others to get the response I desire. I have enough faith in God that things will work out as they should, which is not always the way I want. I turned my worries over to God, but I still kept a close eye on the situation.

I made another trip later that month, again breaking my rule, but I was so worried about Steven having those seizures. It was a week before Christmas, and Matthew and Tina were being evicted from their apartment because Meme was creating too many disturbances with other renters. Luckily for them, I drove my pickup truck that day. I spent the day moving their belongings to a garage for storage at an apartment they would be able to move into on January 1. They said they didn't know where they would be staying for the rest of December. They refused to consider going to the Salvation Army. Meme had already been through there several times, but because she had not complied with their policies, Meme thought they wouldn't let her return. As we were having a very mild winter, I suspected they were making plans to sneak into that garage at night to sleep. I suggested that I could take Steven home with me. I had previously had him for three- and four-day visits at least once a month to give his parents a break. I had bought a small dresser just for his things and always had a supply of anything I would need for his care. It was thus just a matter of my taking him home that day.

But the first day Steven was in my home he had a series of intense seizures. Twice that first day, he had episodes, clusters of inward pulling of his limbs. His little face scrunched up as if he was in pain. He made no noises during the seizures, other than loudly expelling air from his lungs as his body relaxed when the seizure ended. I had never felt so helpless as I did that day. I knew there wasn't anything I could do to stop or lessen the intensity of the seizures. Although the baby made no noises, I heard myself making retching sounds as my body strained with each inward pull of his body. I counted eighteen clusters in the first episode and twenty-three in the second, I immediately called the hospital and talked to his doctor, explaining what I observed and asking if perhaps his heart medication could be causing his difficulties. The doctor thought it was probably nothing serious and suggested I make an appointment if I noticed another episode.

That poor baby. I was also having premenopausal symptoms, one of those classic can't-make-a-simple-decision bad days. It was the kind of day familiar to even the best and brightest of premenopausal women, one that makes them feel like they're losing their sanity. On his second day with me (Benjamin was on the road again), Steven had two more clusters of seizures, followed by another on the third. That's when I called Jackie. I didn't have a clue where Matthew and Tina were, nor how to find them. I didn't know if I could even take Steven to a hospital on my own to have him examined. With Jackie's help, I figured out that I could go to Matthew's job site, talk to him there, and find out where they were staying. Then I could go get Tina and have her come with me to get Steven examined. I intended to set this plan in motion the next morning.

That evening, Tina called to say they were at the Salvation Army shelter. She said that she hadn't told them she had a baby, but now she was missing Steven so much, she wanted me to bring him to her. The next morning, I took him back to his parents and Meme, along with very detailed notes of what he had eaten in the three days he was with me, how he responded to eating, his sleep patterns, his crying sessions and intensity, his bowel movements, and my notes on his seizure activity, temperature, pulse, and anything else I thought that the doctor would want to know.

When I arrived at the Salvation Army shelter, Matthew was at work, so I made certain the director was present to witness and verify what I told Tina and Meme. I explained that Steven was having seizures. I told them they must get Steven to a doctor immediately. I offered to take them. I handed Tina my notes and told her that everything the doctor would want to know was written down for him. Meme assured me and the director that Steven had never displayed the symptoms I was describing when he was in their care. Tina reinforced what she said.

"*What?*" I wondered if any of them—Matthew, Tina, or Meme—had ever noticed the baby's petite seizures, which I had seen the previous month. Had they seen his progression to obviously severe episodes? I doubted he had progressed to such intense episodes just on the day I brought him home with me. When Tina began suggesting (again) that they give Steven to Social Services, I began worrying that she'd become negligent in caring for him as a way to get Matthew to agree to give him up. Were these three so-called adults in his life so self-centered that none of them noticed a baby having seizures? Then the shelter director began laughing and wanted to know how I thought I could diagnose seizures. Tina told me she had to get to her new job, and since I had made her late, maybe I could drop her off on my way back through town. Meme, who was holding the baby, again assured the director that Steven would be fine in her care and that there was nothing to be concerned about. I dropped Tina off at her new job and went home.

As soon as I got home, I called Jackie and told her about my bizarre day. Then I sat down and wrote my second letter to the Social Services Department, in which I described the seizure activity I had observed and expressed my concerns that Steven wasn't going to get help. Even the director at the Salvation Army shelter seemed uninterested in the baby's welfare. Again, I asked them to monitor the family.

Two days later, Matthew called me. He was upset. They had observed the seizure activity, and Tina and Meme were claiming that I had somehow hurt the baby, and that was why he was having these episodes. Tina had taken Steven to the doctor, and again he said it was nothing more than colic. Matthew said Tina and Meme were building a lawsuit against me.

Matthew was also upset because he was being restricted from having any contact with Steven at the Salvation Army shelter. He had checked Steven's diaper for wetness, and because he patted the diaper, then looked inside, another resident had reported him for sexually abusing his son. As a precaution, he was not to have physical contact with Steven. *How much crazier can this world get?* What was also difficult for me to understand was that Tina and Meme found this accusation somehow amusing.

Tina eventually tried to sue the doctors and hospitals for medical neglect and an incorrect diagnosis. She obtained copies of all of Steven's medical transcripts to give to her lawyers. Because of her carelessness, however, I gained possession of those transcripts after her lawyers studied them, and I was able to confirm Tina had taken Steven to be examined when she told me she had, and each time the doctor had attributed the baby's difficulties to colic. After I took Steven to the Salvation Army shelter, Tina reported to the doctor that Steven's complications were caused by something which happened while in the care of his paternal grandmother. There were accusations that I had not fed Steven while he was in my care, as the same amount of food was returned to Tina as she had sent with him. As I read these medical documents, it confirmed my suspicions that Tina was putting more thought into constructing a lawsuit with the aid of medical documentation than getting help for her baby. Tina insisted she knew nothing and suspected that I had done something to hurt Steven. There was no mention of "stupid faces" she admitted to me as having seen in November. She failed to mention the notes I had given her. She failed to state that everything had been clearly written down to be given to a medical professional.

I do not feel the attending physician was in any way medically negligent. I also understood his reaction to my call for help when I was watching the baby having seizures. The doctor I called had never met me. Steven's doctors were dealing with a mother and a grandmother who themselves had long medical histories and who seemed to thrive on legal and medical attention, the latter abetted by medical cards entitling them to free care. Tina once went to the emergency room to have a pierced earring removed. She and her mother are people who have made medical emergencies out of gas cramps. Why would a doctor suspect there would be anything wrong with their baby? That they were not manufacturing more phony emergencies?

After Matthew's phone call, I thought it best if I backed off until the doctor could find the cause of Steven's seizures. Matthew promised he'd call as soon as they knew what was wrong. But although I backed off from my son and his family, I didn't back away from the problems. I prayed. I prayed *fervently* for God to please protect my grandson. This was when I called Jackie, and she started the nationwide prayer chain for God's will regarding Steven's health and that his parents might be able cope with whatever was God's will.

I turned my worries and fears over to the care of God, but when three weeks passed and I still hadn't heard anything, I wrote Matthew a note asking him to please call me. Surely by now, I said, they knew I hadn't done anything to cause the seizures. I mailed the note to the address where they had stored their furniture. It was January, and they would be living there by now. Matthew called me the evening he got the note. He said that just that day, Tina had taken Steven to the doctor's office again, and he'd had a seizure while there. He had been transported by ambulance to a hospital quite a distance away to receive better care for a diagnosis of infantile spasms. Had my son called me during those weeks when Steven went untreated, I would have suggested that they just go and sit in the doctor's office until he had another seizure. After all, he had at least two clusters a day just in those three days when he was with me, which meant they wouldn't have had to wait very long at the office. They would have gotten help so much sooner. What I have never been able to understand is how they could have been living at the Salvation Army shelter, and no one, neither a worker nor another resident, ever suggested that they get help.

From the medical notes for Steven's admission for infantile spasms, I learned that Tina had again neglected to mention the mild seizure activity I had pointed out to her in November. She placed the onset of seizures at five minutes after being dropped off by the paternal grandmother. Tina had told the doctor that while Steven was in my care she had called and asked how the baby was doing. She claimed that she heard him crying in the background, that she demanded that the paternal grandmother to return him to her care. I had been reported as being very rude and angry with the baby, that I had allowed him to cry for more than five hours without trying to comfort him. The only way Tina would have known that Steven cried for five hours and *could not* be comforted was by reading my notes, which were very complete, but which she never mentioned.

Infantile spasms are seizures occurring in babies, usually beginning between three and twelve months of age. They are uncommon, affecting only one baby out of a few thousand. About 60 percent of the spasming infants have some brain disorder or brain injury before the seizures begin, but others have no apparent injury and had previously been developing normally. The cause of Steven's seizures has never been determined, which is often the case. There is plenty of medical evidence that family history, the baby's sex, or factors such as immunizations are not related to infantile spasms. There is contradictory evidence linking vaccinations to infantile spasms, specifically the DPT immunization. Steven received his first dose on September 20, his second on November 15, 1996. This is consistent with when I first noticed the petite seizures. His eyes rolled back and his body stiffened slightly, and he pulled his arms in and his knees up and whimpered. He had four or five of these seizures per episode in the beginning, each lasting a second or two; these clusters are typical of infantile spasms. When I took him home on December 18, he was having intense seizures of eighteen to twenty-three seizures per episode. All medical transcripts state that medical professionals observed four or five per episode, which is consistent with Tina's count.

Steven's seizures were treated with a steroid therapy, ACHT, with some success. After he was released from the hospital, a visiting nurse observed seizure activity when she visited his home to give him his dose of ATCH. She counted twenty-three seizures in that episode. Depakote then was given simultaneously with the ATCH. The last observed seizure occurred when Steven was eight months old, four months after my first observation of his petite seizure. According to Tina, he had been making "stupid faces" before then. As I write this, Steven has remained seizure-free, although many children who suffered infantile spasms will later develop other types of epilepsy.

Most children who suffered infantile spasms are mentally delayed later in life. Those who had an injury or underlying brain disorder have a higher likelihood of moderate to severe retardation. Ten to twenty percent of those who were functioning normally before the onset of spasms will have normal mental functions, whereas others may be only slightly impaired. There is a reference in Steven's medical transcripts that his autistic tendencies may be secondary to the infantile spasms, but I know in my heart that I observed those tendencies shortly after his birth with his rubbing of my knuckles.

Matthew has been adamant that the immunizations are the reason for all of Steven's complications, the seizures, and the autism, even though I have reminded him many times that the hand rubbing was there at ten days old.

Tina's medical lawsuit centered on medical neglect by the original doctor who first claimed Steven's discomfort was colic. These spasms are indeed sometimes misdiagnosed as colic because the seizures look like cramping. But colic doesn't occur in a series. She and Matthew also pursued an immunization connection. However, according to the attorney who considered her suit, although there was some indication of medical neglect, he felt parental cause and neglect were contributing factors. He declined the case, saying it would be too costly and unlikely to succeed.

I became aware from the documents the lawyers reviewed that Steven's safety was in question if he were left alone in his father's care. Tina reported that Matthew was too irresponsible to even change the baby's diaper. I started making those unannounced visits I had promised. I liked to show up at unexpected times, and one of those times was just before Matthew came home from work. Because of what I saw then, in future visits, I made sure to arrive minutes before he got home. When Matthew came home from work, he didn't get a drink of water or soda from the refrigerator, or go to the bathroom to wash or relieve himself. He didn't do anything but walk into the house, go directly to the stack of diapers, and immediately change Steven's diaper. He never checked first if the baby needed changing, he just did it. After watching this a few times, I pointed out the pattern.

"Well," Matthew said, "I know he's going to need changing."

"Yes," I said. "But do you understand what that implies, *knowing* that he needs changing?"

"Yeah," he said. "It means he hasn't been changed all day. I know that."

End of discussion.

I learned from the transcripts that even during Tina's pregnancy Social Services was involved in the prenatal care. When Tina and her newborn were released from the hospital, Social Services was to supervise and see that the baby was properly cared for. I wasn't aware of this until after I read the transcripts. Although the maternal grandmother (Meme) was known to be living with them, it was thought that she probably wasn't any more knowledgeable than the young mother about how to properly care for a child. When Steven was released from the hospital for the infantile spasms, a visiting nurse would come several times a week to give him the shots to control his seizures. I became aware at that time that Social Services was to be involved in teaching Tina how to care for and play with her son.

For the next several months, my visits with Steven took place in my automobile as we drove to the distant hospital for EEGs, doctor visits, and follow-ups. Because Matthew and Tina didn't have a car, I volunteered to take Steven to his appointments. That way, I would always know what the prognosis was and what was being recommended. I didn't trust the explanations Tina gave me, and I soon discovered my suspicions were correct when we returned from an appointment: even Matthew was being kept in the dark as to the results of these medical visits. He was home from work one day when we returned, and when he asked Tina what the doctor had said, she brushed him off. When he asked her again, she told him blatant lies while I was standing there! Because Matthew saw the look on my face, he asked, "What's going on?" and she basically told him it was none of his business. Tina's response when I asked what Social Services did when they made their visits was making more and more sense to me. What she said was, "Oh, just a bunch of stupid shit. They take out these stupid toys and shake them at him. They are just a bunch of dumb assholes who don't know anything."

Okay. During the last appointment, the doctor had talked with Tina about how important it was that Social Services remain involved in helping her with the baby's care. The doctor told Tina that she had been contacted by Social Services in regard to their difficulty in working with Steven, as the family was gone each time they came for their appointments. I made a mental note of the next appointment the doctor scheduled for Social Services to visit; my next visit would coincide with the next social worker's visit. I wanted to see how they were working with Steven. I was back to being allowed having him for home visits, and I wanted to work with him as instructed. When I arrived, I found a note taped to the door from Social Services: "Sorry I missed you." I must have crossed paths with the worker in the parking lot as she was leaving and I was pulling in. I walked right into the apartment, the note taped to my finger now, and found Tina hiding on the back patio, shushing Steven to "be quiet."

From the transcripts, I saw that Tina had been advised at every doctor visit to have Steven enrolled in the Birth-to-Three Program, where he could have been helped. The earlier the intervention for babies who have suffered infantile spasms, the more success there is in helping them overcome mental delay hurdles. Just parental interaction, of which Steven was getting so little, would have helped him. That's what Social Services would have tried to teach Tina. The workers from Birth-to-Three even offered to visit Steven's home to work with him if his parents were having difficulty bringing him to their offices. But Tina would have no part of it. Steven has been, and continues to be, so grossly delayed. If she had allowed supportive home care workers in from the beginning, he could have been helped so much. Someone other than me would have noticed the petite seizure activity.

Matthew and Tina openly laughed when they saw anyone with an obvious physical or mental disability. It was embarrassing to take them anywhere. After Steven's seizures were controlled, the doctors explained that he would suffer mental delays, which is why Birth-to-Three was so strongly recommended. More than a few times I heard Matthew tell Tina, "We better be more careful what we say about the retarded. We have one of our own now, you know."

Once Tina decided she no longer wanted the responsibility of a baby, nothing was going to convince her that it was too late to change her mind. She had a simple solution. "You just give him to Social Services." Not that she allowed Social Services to help her with her child, but when he wasn't fun anymore, they could just take him. Although Meme was living with them, she was determined that she wasn't going to take care of Steven, either. Tina could do it. He was her baby.

Tina resisted anyone who tried to make her take care of the baby. That's why Steven's diapers weren't changed all day. "If Matthew wants him, let him change the diapers," she'd say. Whenever I made my unannounced visits, I never saw Tina or Meme holding Steven; he was either sitting in a baby chair or lying on the floor in front of the TV. I never saw them interact with him. Steven's head is flat in the back from always lying or sitting in a chair and so rarely being held.

One of Steven's earliest survivor skills was his refusal to hold his own bottle at feeding time. He would not drink it if it was propped up for him, either. I think in his own tenacious way, he was demanding that they at least hold him long enough to give him his bottle of milk. When it came to feeding time, Tina chased him around the house with a jar of baby food and a spoon. She never sat him in a chair. The spoon would be heaped with food, so when she caught him, she poked it in and his mouth was full.

When Steven was two, his parents took him to the doctor for what they described as loud and uncooperative behavior. They stated they had lost two apartments because of his long crying spells. My observation of Steven from that time was that he loved being outside. When he was at my home, I took him for long walks in the stroller. To teach him to walk, I bought a Red Flyer wagon and put his hands on the back of the wagon. I pulled, and he had to walk. As tiny as he was, there were times he happily walked a mile, though other times, it was much shorter distances before he wanted to get in and ride. When I took Steven home with me, it was usually at least a four-day visit, sometimes up to nine days. The first couple of days, he slept for long periods of time. Usually, if I laid him down for a nap at 3:00 p.m., I almost expected him to sleep through the night until 8:00 or 9:00 a.m. the next morning. If he woke up, I had a diaper and a dish of graham crackers ready.

I changed his diaper, added milk to the crackers, and fed him, and he went right back to sleep. As the days went on, he adjusted, taking naps in the afternoon and sleeping through the night.

Steven did not live in a happy home. It was full of rage and constant arguments. Meme continued to live with them, and she drank beer. Because her health is so poor, it doesn't take much alcohol to intoxicate her, and when she becomes intoxicated, she rants and raves. At full volume. The language of all three of these adults is peppered with vulgarities. I understood Tina much better than she wanted me to; I, too, had been young and addicted to alcohol. I had been unhappy in a relationship and mother to a son. When Tina had to exert any energy, like, to get up from a chair and get Steven a bottle or to do anything else, she always breathed out a "God damn it." I understood. I've been there, done that.

Tina was provocative and smart. When she wanted to get Matthew out of her life for a while, she provoked him into pushing her away. She would lean into his face and taunt him until he pushed her face away with the palm of his hand, then she ran to the phone and called the police, saying he abused her. She always made certain she wasn't hurt. I provoked men to hit me, too. If they got angry enough to hit me, it meant they cared; otherwise, they would have just walked away. Tina acted like this because she knew Matthew would end up in jail for a bit, and then she could date a hot new boyfriend. After one of these periods of freedom she manipulated for herself, she continued bringing her boyfriend home, even after Matthew was back. The guy walked into the house while Matthew was sitting there and reached out to Steven and said, "Hi, Steven. Come to Daddy." That is just one example of how dysfunctional their home was. This boyfriend didn't stick around long, about three weeks, but it was longer than most of her other boyfriends.

I wondered about Steven's sensitivity to the anger and disharmony around him. One evening when I had him, I lay with him on the bed, waiting for him to fall asleep. My dogs were in the next room, and the older dog, Missy, growled at her pup, Prince Albert, warning him in a very low growl that he was getting too close to her space. Steven's body tightened with fear. I could tell he was waiting for whatever he thought would come next. I explained to him that it was okay. Missy was just telling Albert to move over. Steven then relaxed. I had my answer. He was acutely tuned in to the disharmony in his family. I also observed that he had very acute hearing.

I always worried that Steven was not being cared for lovingly, that he was being neglected and, most likely, abused. If Tina, Matthew, and Meme talked to each other as they did, wouldn't they talk to Steven that way, too? On Easter week, I took Steven home with me on Friday. His parents were to pick him up Easter Sunday at my sister's home, where we planned an Easter meal.

Steven was tired, and I laid him on my sister's bed, where he napped while we ate. I could see that Tina was upset that I laid him down for a nap. She told Matthew she was worried he wouldn't sleep that night. This was when Steven was two, and they were concerned about him not sleeping enough. What she said then told me that they were keeping him up all day, thinking he'd sleep better at night. As most parents know, that just isn't the case: an overtired baby has disrupted sleep patterns. Living in a violent home wasn't helping his sleep patterns, either. We were all preparing to leave my sister's when Tina went in and slid Steven off the bed to wake him up. He was standing on his feet before he even knew he was being awakened from a nap. Then, while he was standing there, just waking up, Tina began shoving heaping spoonfuls of mashed potatoes and gravy into his mouth. He ran away, but she grabbed him, picked him up, and *threw* him on the couch screaming, "You stupid little fucker!"

Tina was upset with me to begin with, and I think she acted this way in front of the rest of the family before she realized what she was doing. But I suspected this was how Steven was being treated at home all the time. Benjamin, my sister's family, and I were so upset by this treatment that we all sat, speechless, in the living room after they left. It was half an hour before Benjamin felt calm enough to drive home, and even then he ran a stop sign on a corner he was very familiar with.

When Steven was three, Tina and Matthew enrolled Steven in the Head Start Program, and for a short time he attended on a sporadic basis. I visited the center, where I could watch through a mirrored window and observe how they were working with him. One day, they were teaching him to feed himself. I watched as they had him hold his own spoon. Sometimes the teacher had to hold her hand over his to keep him from dropping it. She then helped him scooping up his food, either hand over hand, or by lightly placing her hand, palm up, under his forearm and guiding him. When Steven was home with me, I used the prompts I saw being used at Head Start. He could feed himself! When I took him to his home, I sat him down over and over and showed Tina and Meme that he could feed himself with the correct prompts. Tina still chose to chase him around the house with heaping spoonfuls of food.

Steven made few attempts to talk. I usually had him home alone with me while Benjamin was over the road. But one day when Benjamin was home and he had stepped outside, Steven managed to say, "Pa. Pa," while insistently patting my leg. He wanted to be outside with his grandpa. Steven rarely smiled or laughed, but at least while he was in our home, he generally had a contented look about him. This failure to smile or laugh was corrected when he was four years old and had dental surgery. The dentist capped all his teeth, as they were decaying from lack of oral hygiene, and it hurt to open his mouth.

Steven was always so observant. I wondered if he understood what was appropriate and what wasn't. I believe babies are born knowing right from wrong; how else would they know when to cry or show hurt expressions on their face when being treated harshly? I was curious if he understood the difference between the vulgarities he heard in his home and the appropriate language I always tried to use around him. I got my answer to that one day while driving him home from a visit. I was driving our pickup truck and had his car seat in the passenger's seat. He was three at the time. He was sitting with his little legs crossed at the ankles and his arms resting on the front ledge of the car seat, looking quite contented. Just then, another motorist pulled over to the side of the street and swung his car door open. Swerving to avoid hitting him, I exclaimed (I thought under my breath), "Stupid asshole!" Steven looked at me, his mouth wide open in surprise. He then gave the biggest belly laugh, looking at me and shaking his head in disbelief. He had tears rolling down his cheeks, he was laughing so hard. He slowed down, but then he looked over at me and started in all over again. After a few miles, he stopped laughing, but his mannerisms clearly said he had a secret about his grandma. He looked over at me periodically, with the most knowing smile, and shook his head. It was as if I had a sixteen-year-old, not a three-year-old, who had heard his grandma swear for the first time.

In Steven's medical transcripts, there are several references to autistic tendencies beginning from age two. It wasn't until his parents took him to the emergency room for cold symptoms when he was three and a half, however, that either parent actually *heard* someone say Steven had autism. The treating doctor said he had worked on an autism ward for the past eight years. "And this boy is autistic," he declared. I believe that Matthew and Tina had been informed of that diagnosis in the past, but they suffered from denial syndrome, which prevented them from considering the possibility. I remember them being upset by the emergency room doctor so callously making such a blunt statement. They were very upset that their baby might be autistic and drove to my town to talk to me about it. Of course Tina was spewing threats of a lawsuit against this doctor for shocking them. "There's a better way he could have told us," she said.

When I finally heard that a doctor had observed that Steven had autism (it was not a diagnosis), I contacted an autism research institute for information. Included in the packet they sent me was a page that listed criteria describing autistic behaviors. I identified Steven's limited attempts at speech and repetitive behaviors, such as the knuckle rubbing and rolling of objects. He also tried sitting in toy automobiles, regardless of their size, which was explained as autistically distorted perceptions. He turned pictures over, looking for images on the back, another distorted perception. He sat for long periods of time with telephone books on his lap, the binding pulled near his stomach, continuously running the soft pages of the book past his fingertips, another repetitive behavior. I wasn't so certain these "symptoms" indicated autism and were not attributable to other mental delays. The criteria stated that poor eye contact and being unreceptive to parental cuddling were often prominent in children with autism. Well, that just was not the case with Steven. He was very loving, had wonderful eye contact, and always sought to be held. I felt that Steven displayed some autistic behaviors, but that he was probably on a low scale of autism.

I knew Tina was not coping well with her son's mental delays. She so easily ridiculed anyone who had obvious mental or physical disabilities, and her own son's being retarded was perhaps more than she could bear. What is so paradoxical is that her neglectful, abusive parenting seems to be a major contributing factor in his delays. At three and a half, he was not feeding himself, not even finger foods. He would not try to bite, as in biting into a sandwich. He rarely used any words and made no attempts at dressing or any other personal hygiene. He was not toilet trained, and although he carried a small toy with him if it was given to him, he made no attempts at playing with it. Tina attributed his delays solely to the infantile spasms. She could not seem to comprehend that he could be helped if she would involve him in the therapies that the doctors strongly recommended.

I could always see willingness and ability in Steven that he could progress. Although Tina finally had him attend the Head Start Program, attendance was sporadic and short-term. She did not follow through in working with him. She did not, of course, think she was in need of guidance. This young woman is delusional when it comes to perceptions of herself. That is part of her disability, for which she collects SSI benefits. I wondered how the emergency room doctor's statement that Steven was autistic was ultimately going to sit with Tina once she blew off her threats of suing him for shocking her.

# Chapter 4

## *"Yes, Please."*

I am sure that because he was raised in a single household, Matthew has very strong feelings that parents remain together to raise their child. From the time Tina decided they should give Steven to Social Services, it was a constant battle: Tina trying to convince Matthew to give Steven up, Matthew trying to make Tina be a mother to Steven. But just as she had demanded, schemed, and begged to have a baby, now she was equally adamant about giving the baby up. There were several separations, during which Steven lived with Tina. I gave Matthew many pep talks that he should be the one raising his son. I talked to him about finding good day care, about spending time with Steven and taking him for walks. I told him of my observations that he was the one providing what little care Steven was getting. Nothing did any good. Their separations never lasted long.

A big advantage to Steven's living with Tina was that now along with Tina's and Meme's SSI checks, the boy also qualified for benefits because of his mental delays. I was visiting the day Tina got the letter from Social Security stating that Steven would be receiving benefits. She shook with excitement as she opened the envelope, and when she read the letter, she danced and spun around the room, then collapsed onto the sofa, throwing her head back in laughter. "Those stupid fuckers," she said. "I can't believe they are so stupid.

They are giving Steven SSI checks every month. I can't believe it. Oh, my God. They are so stupid." I couldn't understand why she thought they were so stupid, but Tina definitely thought she had hit the jackpot.

From time to time Meme also moved out. There is something very odd in that Meme and Tina cannot seem to live with—or without—each other. Over the years, I have watched one or the other move out, only to have the other one "visiting" so often that pretty soon they decide to live together again and split the expenses.

It has always boggled my mind how Mathew not only stayed in that relationship, but kept returning to it after their separations. Tina and her mother live in a world all their own, full of self-importance and their own rules. The contrast between Matthew's tolerance to them and their desires versus his feelings about me was incredible. I simply requested he take care of himself and occasionally asked him to help me. They demanded he take care of them like the proper queens that they were, and what he didn't give them, they took from him. I have a journal filled with my expressions of disgust, bewilderment, and pain concerning my son's involvement with them. The drug and alcohol addictions and the craziness surrounding their personalities were maddening.

I could see that much of his attraction in this extremely dysfunctional lifestyle was their brazen disrespect for society in general. It seemed as though his association with them was a defiant act against me. He still had all his childhood grievances stacked up. In his first years with Tina and Meme, during the few occasions when Matthew visited me alone, he would laugh and tell me about their talent for getting free stuff, as when Tina walked through the kitchen appliance section of a store, grabbed a coffee pot off the shelf, tore the lid a little, and then took it to the service counter to "exchange it for cash, as it was a gift and we already have a nice coffee pot." Another time, she put a large vacuum cleaner under the shopping cart, paid for a small item, and walked out with the vacuum cleaner without paying for it. Then she drove to another town fifty miles away to return it for cash at the same franchise.

Despite all the confusion in their household, Tina and Meme were meticulous about keeping their receipts for items they purchased. I have seen exercise equipment used for several months, then out came the receipts and back to the store it went. Even Steven's first playpen, which they used for at least a year, was packed up, the sales receipt taped to the box, and taken back to the store. They used stores as free rental sites, places to get quick cash when they felt they needed it. Obviously, at least in the beginning, Matthew was greatly intrigued by their boldness and cleverness at acquiring pretty much whatever their hearts desired, especially in contrast to my scrimping and saving.

What I could never understand was when they stole from Matthew, it was just a fact of life. I know he often slept with his pants on and his wallet in his pocket, trying to keep them from lifting money while he slept. But he's a sound sleeper, and they just took the money and slipped the wallet back into his pocket. His employers told me they had seen Tina hiring a cab to take her to Matthew's work site, a good fifteen-mile ride. They watched her take a partial pack of cigarettes out of Matthew's car, then take the cab home again. She did this more than once. It was her way of teaching him not to leave her home without cigarettes. They lived about a mile from a store. Steven would have loved a stroller ride and some fresh air.

Matthew seemed to accept all of this inappropriate behavior as just the way life was. I didn't notice that he had much of a desire to get out of the situation, nor did he ever try to make his life a little more worthwhile. When raising him, I certainly tried to teach him respect for himself and others, but it was those beliefs of mine that he especially pooh-poohed. As far as he was concerned, my philosophy of life was where I was the most stupid. He thought I didn't know what I was talking about. I could tell he didn't like his living situation with Tina and Meme, but it was something he felt he had to tolerate.

Over and over, I asked Matthew why he stayed in such a sick relationship. The answer was always Steven. Finally, when Steven had just turned four, Tina packed as much stuff of his and Matthew's as she could push into the car, wrote out what she felt was a legal-enough document saying that Matthew now had full custody of their son Steven (and it was legal enough), and told them to get the hell out of there. Not knowing what else to do, or who would help him with his son, Matthew drove straight to our house. "What can I do?" he asked me.

Because it was still summer, Benjamin and I told Matthew he could camp out in a tent in our yard and that Steven could stay in the house with me. Within a few days Matthew found employment with a local landscaping company. We thought it a good idea that on nights when Matthew didn't have to work the next morning, that Steven could camp with his daddy. We also told Matthew that I would help with the babysitting while he worked, but that it was conditional on his studying and completing his High School Equivalency Diploma (GHED).

Benjamin and I felt we were back to the basics with Matthew in the tent in our backyard. He came to us broke, and, quite honestly, we weren't sure this breakup would last any longer than the others. I had given him furniture in the past, only to find it on the curb when he and Tina got back together. I was past giving him money. All I would offer now were support and guidance and good child care.

Where he was going to live came up for discussion. When he first came, I told him he had to call Social Services, tell them about his situation, and ask for early childhood schooling for Steven. I told him to ask where the best schooling was, and Social Services told him the school district Benjamin and I were living in was "by far the best." I already knew this, but I also knew how Matthew never believed anything I had to say. He always had to hear it from someone else. He still wanted to argue with me and said he didn't want to live in our community. "Listen," I said. "You said I'm the one you want helping with Steven. If you live somewhere else, that means I'll be doing all the driving to pick him up and to drop him off. You have babysitting services with me for free. You can at least do the transporting."

I was fighting for two things here. First, I wanted the best schooling we could get for Steven. He had been denied decent schooling for far too long. Second, my intuition was screaming at me again. I kept having visions of returning Steven to his daddy's home and not having anyone home. I was being strongly advised to wait for Matthew in the comfort of my own home.

Regardless of earlier efforts by the doctors and Social Services to have Steven involved in developmental programming, when Matthew tried to enroll him in early childhood education, he mentioned the emergency room doctor's statement that Steven had autism. There was never a diagnosis of this written in his medical history, only references to "autistic tendencies." To register Steven in early childhood, Matthew needed a diagnosis. It was in fall of 2000, when Steven was four years old, that his evaluation was completed. The diagnosis was autism, with mental delays a secondary factor.

One evening, while Matthew was still camping in our yard, he came home from work while Steven was finishing his supper, and we all sat around the table, visiting. Although Steven spoke very few words, he had said "shoe" earlier in the day for me, and Matthew and I began trying to get him to say it again. "Say 'shoe,'" Matthew said several times, and then Steven got a devilish grin on his face and clearly said, "Boot!" Then he laughed the most beautiful laugh at his joke. That was our introduction to Steven's delightful sense of humor. I was relieved by his word association; it told me he had the ability for cognitive thought.

Matthew hadn't been camping in our yard for two weeks when Meme called me to say she had moved to the town where Matthew said he wanted to live. She didn't know where Matthew and Steven were staying, and I sure didn't tell her they were with me, but she knew I knew where they were. She wanted to know when she could visit with Steven. After that, I had at least one phone call a day reminding me that she had rights, too, and she was demanding to see Steven. Finally, Matthew caved and took Steven to visit her. Not two weeks later, Tina called looking for Matthew. She had apparently moved in with her mother. Then I started getting several phone calls a day. "Where is Matthew?" "When will Matthew be home from work?" "Is Matthew there yet?" Tina convinced him that she really missed Steven. "Could I please see him?" So Matthew took Steven to her, and then she'd think of something she needed and suggest they leave Steven with Meme while they went elsewhere. Tina seemed to want Matthew, not Steven.

Next, Matthew began taking Steven to Meme's almost every weekend. My problem with this was that I was trying to potty train my grandson, to let him feed himself, and to keep him outside for some much-needed fresh air. Steven was registered in the early childhood program now and going to school half days during the week. I took care of him for the rest of the day while his daddy worked. Neither Meme nor Tina ever made any attempt to try potty training Steven, nor did they let him feed himself when he was with them. Each Monday, therefore, I started over from the beginning. Eventually I learned that these women were *demanding* that Matthew take Steven to them and he kept caving in. I overheard him tell them on the phone that he had some rights too, and because he was working all week, he didn't get to see Steven much, whereas they had him every weekend. Matthew said he wanted Steven for a weekend. I have realized over and over that that boy of mine just isn't too smart.

The most frustrating thing for me was that whatever I told Matthew was just a bunch of garbage, yet these two women had him jumping through hoops. As he got older, however, he began respecting my opinion and started asking for suggestions to help him make decisions. But Tina and Meme could wipe out any sound, reasonable decisions he made in a matter of seconds. He always stood up to me. Why wasn't he able to stand up to them?

Matthew found a studio apartment in our community and did reasonably well at working and getting Steven to and from school. Steven's teachers always commented that Steven was clean and that there was never any evidence of rashes or other telltale signs that his diapers weren't being changed. They could see that Matthew was taking good physical care of Steven. The teachers did, however, question Steven's strange attempts at feeding himself. He heaped his spoon and shoved his mouth full of food. He was feeding himself the way he had been fed. It was how he thought he was supposed to eat.

Matthew studied and completed his GHED commitment, except for the math. Math is a real weakness of his. He had been living near us for almost two years before he actually took time off from work to attend a math class at the local technical school. It was a series of four-hour sessions, five days a week. Come on! He had been "studying" for a month, and it didn't sound to me like he was any closer to passing the test than when he first started the class. Given the fact that I was babysitting for eight hours a day as if he had a job that lasted eight hours, I asked him, "What gives?" I really wanted to know. I wasn't getting any of my spring yard work done because I was babysitting all the time. Matthew showed me that I had no right to ask him what the hell was up; he stopped bringing Steven over. It wasn't any of my damned business what he was doing, even if I was babysitting while he did whatever he did.

Matthew and Tina had decided to get back together, and he wasn't eager to share his good news with me. They were playing house and taking advantage of me. He showed me that I shouldn't interfere in his life by keeping Steven away from me and refusing to call me. This went on for perhaps a month; I got a lot of gardening done during that time. While I was whacking and weeding, of course, I was symbolically whacking the devil out of Matthew. Was I ever going to be able to reach him? *Whack.* Would he ever change the course of his miserable life? *Whack.*

Eventually, I called Matthew and invited him and Steven for a family picnic. They came. Although I had Steven urinating on the toilet, after about a month of being with his mother, he was no longer using the toilet. Steven had been talking, too, but now he was jabbering again. He had been feeding himself, but here, too, he had regressed. I was devastated. He was now six years old. Any parent or guardian raising a mentally disabled child, much less one with an autism diagnosis, too, knows that these children take a lot more patience, instruction, and coaxing than most other children require. To see these regressions in every area where progress had been gained was heartbreaking for me. He had been so proud of his accomplishments, and now they were gone. My not-too-smart son didn't seem to connect the regressions with Tina. I think he really did, though; ignoring his son's welfare was apparently the price he was willing to pay to have Tina back in their lives.

I couldn't keep watching them neglect Steven. But I couldn't just kick them out of our lives. I kept hoping that one day he would be able to somehow remember having done these things for himself. I kept hoping he would just tell his mother, "No." When Tina fed Steven, she didn't even give him time to swallow what he had before she was shoving more in his mouth. I hoped that one day he would grab the spoon and feed himself in a dignified manner.

Benjamin was also having a hard time with Steven's regressions and obvious neglect. What made it especially difficult was that, although Steven was mentally disabled, there was no way to predict how self-sufficient he might become. He never spent enough time in a structured, stable environment to get a true test of his development without Matthew giving into Tina's demands and taking Steven back to her. There was, however, clear evidence that progress could be made.

Without my knowing it, Benjamin began attending mobile church services at truck stops when he was working out of town on weekends. In fact, he began planning his trips so that he would be working weekends and be able to attend these services. Because so few people attend them, he was able to have private sessions with the ministers. The third minister he talked to convinced him that *someone* had to take proper care of Steven and that, clearly, the parents were unprepared to handle him themselves. It wasn't the child's fault. Someone had to step in and give him the stability he needed. Regardless of Benjamin's belief that everyone had to be responsible for their own choices and behavior, this minister assured him that some parents cannot be forced into doing the responsible thing. All of our guidance and support of Matthew's raising Steven supported our belief in responsibility, because I am of the same mindset.

I was absolutely flabbergasted, therefore, when Benjamin came home from that trip and informed me that he felt we needed to take guardianship of Steven. When I wrote the letter to Social Services, I was thinking of a six-month placement, but Benjamin was talking permanent guardianship, or guardianship until either one of his parents made necessary changes to take back their parental obligations. In reality, we were probably looking at permanent placement. I didn't just jump up and say, "Oh, yes, darling"; "Come on, dear, this is quite a commitment we are looking at," is more like it. We discussed it, and it really was all about Steven. It had become obvious in the two years that they had lived in this area, where we were able to observe more closely the dysfunction in the relationships of Matthew, Meme, and Tina, that if we didn't step in, Steven would never function in any self-sufficient capacity. If he were not provided with a more stable, structured environment, we would never know what he was capable of doing.

When we made the decision to talk to Matthew about our taking guardianship, Steven was spending the night with us. He was still just jabbering, not back to using words yet. That night as I was tucking him into bed, I told him that Grandpa and I were thinking that maybe he should come and live with us at our house. He sat up in bed, looked me straight in the eye, and said, "Yes, please." Steven's response was perfect, when for weeks he had been only jabbering. I wasn't sure he understood what I'd said, so I repeated my statement and added that it meant he would move all his toys, his clothes, and his bed to our house, and that his daddy would only be visiting him. Again he sat up in bed, looked me in the eye, and said, *"Yes, please!"* with such emphasis that there was no doubt he understood what I was saying. This made our decision a lot easier on me, as I had been struggling with the idea of being the one to "take him from his family."

When Matthew came to pick Steven up the next day, I talked to him about our belief that Steven needed more structure in his life and that we wanted him to come live with us. Matthew was visibly relieved. He said he had wanted to talk to us about that very thing, but was finding it difficult to start the conversation. So that went easy enough.

When Benjamin and I built our home, we built it small; we hadn't planned on raising children. We'd had enough foresight, though, to build moveable bookshelf walls so that we could easily resection our home should we ever want to. Now we took two of these moveable bookshelf walls and made a temporary bedroom for Steven off our bedroom. He came to live with us the day he started kindergarten. I went to his father's apartment and we packed all his stuff into my car. Steven turned six years old in July of that year, and there was Tina, spoon-feeding him cereal. From his daddy's, I took Steven to school for his first day of kindergarten. It was the same school where he attended early childhood classes. The decision to keep him in early childhood for full days rather than begin kindergarten had been made the year before.

During the first week of school, the secretary called to say she was sending a pamphlet home with Steven for a Grandparents Support Group. "You're darn right, we're going," Benjamin declared before he even saw the pamphlet. We found the support group to be informative and in a relaxed atmosphere. We have made good friendships with other grandparents. Of course, our grandchildren come to these meetings with us; it's difficult to find babysitters, and many of these children had been left in the care of others too much in the past. While grandparents are engaging in a supportive group discussion, other workers provide structured activities with the grandchildren. Sometimes they make us a meal, set the table, and have everything ready for us. They have also made Halloween and Christmas decorations. After group discussions, we always have a meal, and it is always pizza. Sometimes, instead of discussions, we spend an evening at the water park, where we all go swimming and sit in hot tubs. There are perfect opportunities for individualized discussions in the hot tubs. These meetings are where Benjamin and I got the answers we needed about what course to take with guardianship of Steven. As his legal guardians, we make all decisions for him without regard to his parents' wishes.

Most of the grandparents in our group are raising their grandchildren because of the parents' drug and alcohol problems. A common theme of discussion is how exhausting it is being older and caring for active children. While we often wish things were different, every grandparent in our support group is just as determined as Benjamin and I are to provide loving, stable homes for their grandchildren. After stating our grievances, we start laughing, and then the conversation swings to, "If they think they can take them back home now, they're in for a fight!" Sadly, most parents choose not to make the changes in their lives that would enable them to resume custody of their children. And, no, most of us grandparents are not going to hand over these grandchildren for more abuse and neglect. The parents often separate, find new lovers, and have more children. Seeing their older children becoming responsible, they want them back home so they can help keep the house clean and be useful as babysitters for the new kids. We grandparents aren't going to stand for that.

Before going to court for the final determination of guardianship of our grandson, Benjamin, the parents, and I all had to be interviewed by a guardian *ad litem*, who also inspected our home to be certain that this placement would be in the best interests of the child. The court date for guardianship was December 4, 2002. Both of Steven's parents were there, although Tina didn't have to be, as she had previously given full custody to Matthew. Steven was in school. The attorney we hired was also there, and we had to wait outside the courtroom for one session to finish before we could enter. There were no tears from either parent, no discussion of feelings they may have had about relinquishing their child to someone else. Not a thank-you for relieving them of their responsibilities or for giving their son a good home and a better chance at life. Not even an "I'm sorry" for how this decision of theirs was going to change our lives. Nothing.

My son, who had given his son good physical care, brought along two of his political books. He is obsessed with politics. He's neither liberal nor conservative, but believes that the government is a big conspiracy, full of lies and deceit. There is much written to support his beliefs. I knew that during the time he could have spent with his son in the evenings, he had been studying his political books and left Steven to entertain himself. Now, at this court hearing for placement of his child, it was emotionally devastating to me to see Matthew bring his political books into the courtroom. He intentionally placed them so that the judge could see what he was reading. He was obviously trying to make an impression, to show off his political wisdom rather than face the reality of his choices and behaviors that had made him an unstable parent. I realize that this diversion could have been his way of avoiding very painful feelings, but mostly it was his obsession with politics that caused him to see this courtroom hearing as an opportunity to try to make a political statement.

All Tina said was yes when the judge asked her if she was in agreement with the placement of her son. She seemed very happy that day, eager to get the heck out of there so she and Matthew could get on with their carefree lives. The judge made it very clear that the guardianship decision could be redetermined in the event that either or both parents ever came to a point in their lives that they felt they could resume responsibility for parenting their child. My observation was that neither wanted to concern themselves with that possibility.

So Tina and Matthew rode off into their happy little sunset, while Benjamin and I left the courthouse speechless. Their lack of feeling just blew our minds. But no matter about them. Now we were looking at the reality of some very serious business we had agreed to: raising a mentally delayed child with autism. We had just taken a very big step, and that step would completely change our lives. The magnitude of what this new responsibility meant for us could not be put into words.

The nonreactions of Steven's parents were a strong reassurance to us that we were doing the right thing in taking over guardianship of this wonderful little boy. We were on our way home before we found our voices. When we did begin talking, we found we were united. We would both love and cherish Steven. We would never treat him with the disregard he had experienced so far in his short life.

# Chapter 5

## *"We Need to Go to Church, Grandma."*

To the degree that Matthew was angry, resentful, and belligerent, Steven is loving, forgiving, and gentle. Both have been perplexing for me.

The longer I was sober and seeing life in a different light, the more clearly I saw how desperately my son needed help. He was why I worked so hard at stabilizing my life and finding practical solutions to our problems. Though I changed my life to help him, I didn't get many positive results for my efforts. All the changes I made were good for me, too, of course. None of them were wasted. I will never regret this sober life I chose. I have told Matthew many times that he was my teacher, that he was the one who opened doors for me on my path of life. But if he would just do as I did! I had to learn that each person has to find his or her own way. I couldn't change anyone but myself.

Steven is just as perplexing. He was horribly neglected and abused. He was the "stupid little fucker." I remain truly astonished that Steven is as gentle and kind as he is. He does not use curse words, for example, which boggles my mind. Steven lived with, then had liberal contact with his troubled mother and Meme for the first six years of his life, and that's the only language he ever heard from them. How could he not use curse words? Limited as his language was, he never imitated the language he heard. The three adults in his early life used the most profound vulgarities imaginable. Profanity was the language they spoke, just as English or German or Spanish are spoken in other homes.

Steven knows when he is not being treated with respect. I have witnessed other children at parks and beaches. When they catch on that Steven is "different," and they don't know him, they start teasing him. He just ignores them and goes on about his business as if they aren't there. He won't even make eye contact with them. He knows when adults aren't sincere and spots people who aren't very nice. He will not interact with them. What an intricate child Steven is. He is not stupid. He knows he was neglected and abused. Most children coming from similar backgrounds would emulate the way they've been treated. It's not that they liked being treated that way; they just hadn't been taught any other way to interact. How Steven endured the behaviors from his early childhood, yet refused to replicate them, is utterly amazing to me.

Initially, when Benjamin and I obtained guardianship, we asked Matthew to limit his visits to Sunday afternoons until Steven had a chance to adjust to living with us, however long that adjustment might take. We worried that if his dad visited too often, it would confuse Steven. Neither his mother nor Meme was allowed to visit on our premises. As far as Benjamin and I were concerned, Tina had spent years trying to convince Matthew to "give him up." She didn't want Steven. She refused to be a loving, nurturing mother. But then she wanted liberal visitation. And Meme? She was just too nasty. We couldn't think of any reason to invite these women into our home. Living with us was Steven's opportunity to change his life. He no longer had to be exposed to insane behavior.

Meme seemed determined to make our lives a living hell. She let me know from day one that she had her rights, and just because Steven lived with us now, she wasn't going to be cut out of his life. She started calling every day about two in the afternoon, then every fifteen minutes thereafter until she could talk to Steven. It didn't matter that I told her every day that Steven didn't get home from school until almost four o'clock. The repeated phone calls were her attempts at intruding into our lives. She occasionally tried to assert her "rights," saying she should have weekend visits; after all, I had him all week. When Steven got home from school, I always kept him outside, playing catch or kick ball. When the phone rang, I always ran to answer it, expecting Benjamin, who called home every day when he was over the road. He tried to time his calls when he knew I would have Steven off the bus and we could talk without disruptions. Too often, however, it was Meme or Tina wanting their daily "talks" with Steven. I found this very troubling because

I knew it was probably more verbal contact with him than he'd ever gotten when he was in their care. He wasn't able to have a phone conversation. He still had limited language skills, so they usually asked him to sing one or two of the songs I taught him. When I listened in, I heard them repeating over and over that they loved him, missed him, and wanted to visit him. A lot of it was trying to elicit an "I love you" out of him. They were so darned needy.

Coming home from an outing one Sunday afternoon, Benjamin, Steven, and I received a phone message from a very drunken Meme. Then the phone rang, and we looked at one another wondering if we should pick it up. I said no, that if it was her again, she'll just hang up and call back in fifteen minutes. We let the answering machine take the call; sure enough, there was no message and a quick hang-up. Whenever Tina called trying to find Matthew, she too called every fifteen minutes until she reached him. Sure enough again, fifteen minutes later there was another call, and again the caller didn't leave a message. Right on the dot, the phone rang again fifteen minutes later; no message. During the next fifteen-minute gap, I changed our answering machine message: "Meme, if this is you calling again, sober up and get a life." The next call brought a loud gasp and a quick disconnect. It was several days before she called again.

The insanity of alcoholism was trying to invade our lives, no matter what changes Benjamin and I had previously made to distance ourselves from it. This invasion needed to be stopped. When Meme called again several days later, I told her that she would be allowed one phone call per month and warned her not to abuse that privilege or she would then get no phone calls at all. She believed me. After that, she kept to the one call.

When Steven got home from school at 3:50, I tried to keep him outside for at least an hour. Then it was time for supper, and by six o'clock he was asking to go to bed. At first Benjamin and I tried keeping him up until seven o'clock and worked on teaching him colors, letters, and counting. But that proved to be a bit too late, and a 6:30 bedtime was soon established. He was up at seven the next morning and getting on the bus by 7:35. So we had very few hours to actually spend with our grandson. Benjamin, who was on the road from Monday to Friday, had even less time with Steven, mostly weekends when he was home.

When he was living with his parents and Meme, Steven had rarely had his own room. They lived in one bedroom apartments and moved frequently, usually to other studio apartments. Everyone slept pretty much where they dropped. I remember only one apartment in which Steven had his own room; he turned one year old there. When he moved in with us, he was so proud of his bedroom! It was nothing more than a space for his twin bed against the back of one bookcase wall, plus enough walking room on the other side to get into his bed. To further give him the feel of having his own room, I hung juvenile curtains on another bookshelf wall and a matching juvenile valance between the two bookcase walls at the foot of his bed. For that first year, Steven wanted to show his "very own bedroom" to anyone and everyone who visited our home.

A few months later, when Meme made her monthly call to Steven, she asked me if she'd be able to have visits with him. I try to be fair, regardless of undesirable behaviors in others, but this was very difficult to consider. Meme is a chronic alcoholic, and a foulmouthed one on top of that. I couldn't see any reason to expose Steven to her behavior any more. I was exhausted, feeling overwhelmed with my new responsibilities, and not at all enthusiastic about making arrangements that would take yet more time away from things I wanted to do. I was already having difficulty finding time for myself. So I told her that she could visit only after she had been sober for three months. If she stayed sober for three months, I knew much of the nastiness would drain away. She agreed, and our agreement gave me three more months to adjust to my new obligations. I felt I'd be more willing then to make time for a visit. I promised Meme that I would know if she was indeed sober. Then she called me another afternoon to tell me she was receiving outpatient therapy and who she was seeing. She also told me how many and which AA meetings she was attending and suggested that I call her therapist and confirm her involvement in treatment. She had signed a release saying I could be told she was involved in counseling. She said she had been sober for a month and a half and asked if she would still be able to have a visit with Steven at the three-month mark. The only confirmation I needed was hearing sobriety in the tone of her voice. At the three-month date, I took Steven to a fast-food restaurant to see her. She was indeed sober. But Tina was with her.

I had not put the same sobriety restriction on Tina. There are various reasons for this. Tina is a game player; she would have considered it a game and a challenge to try to put one over on me. I didn't have the energy to get into games with her, and, besides, I thought Steven should see his mother for what she was. I didn't have a problem with that, but I expected that as he got older, if she showed up for visits halfway put together, it would confuse him as to why he wasn't living with her. Tina has never disappointed me. She has never sobered up for visits with her son, and sometimes she's so much under the influence of drugs that her tongue is thick and her speech slurred. Tina always comes with Meme, and Meme at least is sober when she visits Steven. This doesn't mean that Meme remains sober. She just stops drinking periodically to ensure visits with her grandson.

At the time Benjamin and I took guardianship of Steven, I had not gone to church for many years. I feel comfortable in my beliefs. I believe completely in Jesus Christ, in God, and in eternal life. However, I stopped going to church in my early twenties. I realize this seems contradictory. Since my recovery, I am constantly aware of God. I'm in awe of life and grateful for every second of my life and all I have been given. But going to church never made me feel more connected to God. In fact, church was part of my early life with my dysfunctional family. I think that's why I left it behind.

Shortly after Steven moved in with us, and he and I were driving past my childhood church, I mentioned I had gone to that church when I was a little girl. He responded by saying, "Grandma, we need to go to church." This was before he was generally speaking clearly, and if he ever stated any desire correctly, we rewarded him by doing as he requested. For instance, if he suggested that we go for a walk, and his preference was clearly stated, we went for a walk. One day when waiting for the bus to bring him home from school, neither Benjamin or I felt too hungry and agreed we'd have just a light supper meal. Steven got off the bus suggesting that we go to McDonald's. Because he answered, "Eat!" when we asked what we would do there, that's where we went. Now he spoke about going to church with such clarity and conviction that, after my sinking feelings of *Oh, no, no, no,* I said, "Huh? What, honey? What did you say?"

"Grandma, we need to go to church."

After that, Steven and I shopped around, attending Mass at a few churches, then decided to attend services at a nice little church where I felt I'd be comfortable. Now we rarely miss Sunday morning services. As difficult as it has been to teach Steven necessary life skills, I was amazed that after each Sunday service, he sat in the backseat of the car and conducted his own service during the ride home. He held his hands in the air, just like Pastor Sarafin, and asked his congregation, "Pray with me, please." Then he jabbered and made sounds of prayer, then correctly recited the names of those people included on the special prayer list. After many months of doing this every Sunday, I brought along a tape recorder. He apparently understood that I was going to record him, for he refused to conduct Mass that morning and has ever since. In 2004, when he was eight, he stood before the congregation at Christmas Mass and sang the first stanza of "Silent Night" so softly and beautifully that he brought tears to his fellow churchgoers' eyes. The next year he stood before the congregation again and sang another solo of "Silent Night," this time with all three stanzas.

We have invited Pastor Sarafin to our home for lunches and visits. Pastors are very busy people, and ours had to cancel a lunch one day for an emergency. I understood, of course, but I thought it was very odd when

Steven requested that we stay home the next Sunday. I happily rewarded him for his well-spoken request. I really didn't think too much of it, other than it was so nice to have just one day that I could be home for the whole day. It was a nice break. Several months later, Pastor Sarafin had to cancel another lunch date. When Steven suggested that we not go to church again that following Sunday, I caught on to a pattern developing. I asked if he was angry that Pastor Sarafin wasn't able to come to lunch. "Yes," he said. He didn't go to church that Sunday, but I did. I thought Pastor Sarafin should know about Steven's reactions to her cancellations. We have been very careful about lunch plans since then.

When Steven looks at anyone, it sometimes feels as if he's looking into your soul. He seems to be searching for unspoken truths. His eye contact can be so strong that it pulls you into him, though every so often, he'll look over my shoulder and smile or laugh. I finally asked him if someone was standing behind me.

"Yes," he replied.

"Is it my guardian angel?" I asked.

"Yes," with an incredulous tone, as if saying, "Like who else would it be?"

"What color does my angel wear?" I wanted to know.

"Purple," he said. He sounded a bit irritated that I should have to ask.

"What color does your angel wear?"

"Purple!" By this time, he was clearly irritated. He turned and walked away from me, not happy that I wrecked the fun we were having.

What seemed strange to me wasn't that he seemed upset that I questioned what colors the angels were wearing. I think this was his first realization that not everyone sees angels. Since then I talk to him from time to time about not seeing angels myself, but I tell him I feel them close by. The other thing I wondered about from that conversation was why he got so irritated at my asking what colors they wore. I always asked him what colors I was wearing. We were trying to teach him colors.

Because Benjamin was gone during the week, he missed being more involved in Steven's life. He made up for it on the weekends by taking Steven with him wherever he went. That was another change for me; I used to be the one who went with him when he had to go somewhere. But he also saw it as an opportunity to give me a break. I was supposed to go shopping, visit friends, or just stay home in a quiet house while he took Steven out. I tried enjoying the quiet for a while, but I missed being with Benjamin. We had so little time together, and now, even when he was home, we were down to almost no time together. I finally started asking if I could come along, too.

Our love life took a big hit, too. We were afternoon lovers, and I don't think I need to explain how having a young one in need of constant supervision living with us changed that. We didn't have much energy left by the time we went to bed for loving, either.

When Steven first moved in, I felt angry and resentful toward my son and Tina, especially while I was outside waiting for the school bus to bring Steven home. He came home during the time of day that my body was accustomed to relaxing. There were days I was so tired, all I wanted to do was sit down and cry. I felt indignant that Tina and Matthew found it so easy to give Steven up. They had simply given their problem away when they didn't want to be bothered with it anymore. I felt angry that Benjamin and I had to pick up their responsibilities. Once that bus pulled in, however, I always put on my happy face. I was always happy Steven was home. I believe that it's a lot easier to reach children when they know they are loved and that someone is waiting to hear about their day, as if hearing their news is the most exciting thing in the world. After hearing about Steven's day, I involved him in playing outside rather than letting him watch TV. Yes, I could have taken an easier route and turned the TV into his babysitter, but it honestly never crossed my mind to do that. This child was so grossly delayed that I could not meet what I felt was my responsibility halfway. I wanted to do everything I could possibly do to help him. I have no regrets.

Soon Benjamin and I had to build an addition onto our home. Steven's tiny bedroom was okay temporarily, but it was way too close to our bedroom and, as Steven grew, much too small to be considered a permanent arrangement. Steven had joined us in the fall. We saved money through the winter, and the next spring we built an additional bedroom and back entryway. Benjamin's and my bedroom was now upstairs in the new addition, which is also equipped with a whirlpool bathtub. The downstairs bedroom became Steven's and includes a spacious play area for him.

So it took time, but we adjusted to our lives, and we settled into new routines. Steven is a very gentle and kind young boy. Unlike many children with autism who avoid human contact, he has always wanted to sit in our laps and cuddle. Children with autism often avoid eye contact, but this is another issue that is not a concern with Steven. Nor has he ever displayed any of the aggressive behaviors sometimes associated with autism. He has been a very willing participant in changing routines, which is not always the easiest thing for children with autism. He has displayed few tendencies to arrange his possessions "just so," another characteristic behavior associated with autism. Repetition of behaviors, such as the knuckle rubbing, rolling pencils and balls, and echolalia (the repetition of what is said by other people) have, however, been prominent. Some of this was baffling to me. Was he autistic or not?

I began toilet training Steven when he was four and he was with me while his dad worked. Toilet training children doesn't have to be difficult. One method is that on any day when the adult is able to keep a fairly close eye on the child, they slip a pair of training pants on them. Then the adult gives the child lots and lots of their favorite drink. They make it available to them all day long. The adult learns to be quick at recognizing when the child needs to go potty, and it generally takes just a few trips to the toilet, plus a small reward of their favorite treat, before the child begins to grasp the concept of not going potty in their pants. On the second day that I was making beverages available to Steven, he picked up the sippy cup, then set it back down instead of taking a drink. He clearly said, "It'll make me go pee." So much for my foolproof attempt at potty training! I couldn't get him to drink anything for the rest of that day, and very little for the next several days,

Because Steven stayed dry at night, when he woke up in the morning, he and I went directly outside, and I had him walk with me on our secluded property without his pants on. I hoped that when he saw himself urinating, it would help him understand what was happening. He resisted as long as he could, but when he started urinating, it scared him, and he grabbed me and peed on my leg. I was willing to let him pee on my leg if it would help him, but he held back each morning until I became concerned about the damage he could be doing to his bladder by holding it so long. This was another failed attempt at what I thought would be a foolproof method of potty training.

Once Steven moved in with us, however, and I was able to keep a consistent toileting routine, I began having more success. I wouldn't let him wear diapers at home. I watched him like a hawk. When I noticed he was ready to do his business, I led him into the bathroom. What was so frustrating for Benjamin and me was that, despite the success at home, when we asked him, "Will you tell the teachers when you have to go potty at school, so they can help you?" he flat out said, "No." At home, he was walking into the bathroom when he needed to go and going by himself. He was pulling his own pants up and down, all without my asking him if he needed to use the bathroom. I remember telling Benjamin how wonderful it was that Steven was doing this by himself at home.

"Imagine," I said, "at least four times a day, he's doing this himself. Each time when I had to help him, it took at least five minutes. With him going four times a day, that gives me an extra twenty minutes a day!" It was such a relief for me having those extra twenty minutes that I broke down and cried.

Bowel movements on the toilet were a whole lot harder than just urinating. He dumped his load in his diaper at school, apparently so he wouldn't have to deal with it at home where Grandma would ask him to do it on the toilet. It was while he was on Christmas break from school that he held his bowels to the point we worried about impaction. I gave him a child's suppository. Although he asked to use the bathroom, Benjamin and I kept him entertained for at least twenty minutes; otherwise, he would have just pushed the suppository out. After twenty minutes, it took both Benjamin and I to hold Steven on the toilet to let nature take its course. It was horrible for all of us. I was kneeling, giving him a full chest hug to hold him and try to comfort him, and Benjamin was keeping his palms fully extended on Steven's upper legs to keep him from pushing himself off the toilet. We had to do this at least four times before Steven understood that he would feel so much better once he moved his bowels. He was finally using the toilet at home with 100 percent success rate and having no accidents. For the next few years, when he had to use the bathroom he said, "I have a tummy ache," or "Make that tummy ache go away." Our next challenge was to help him learn to say, "I need to use the restroom," so others had a clearer understanding about his "tummy ache."

At school, because Steven did whatever he had to do in his pants, he had to wear a diaper, although he was saving bowel movements for at home business now. Toward the end of the school year, my frustration reached a point where I suggested to his teachers that maybe I could spend three complete days with Steven at school and perhaps get him used to using the toilets there. So off to school I went for potty patrol. But to no avail. For three days, that little darling of mine held his bladder until he got home. This experience convinced me (and everyone else) that he had incredible bladder control. But he wasn't doing his bladder any favors by abusing it, and I decided to see what he would do with this potty business when he started school again in the fall.

As it turned out, the last day of the school year in which I conducted potty patrol was the last time Steven wore a diaper. When he returned from school that day, I took his diaper off and told him how exciting it was that he would never have to wear a diaper again. After the summer vacation, he returned to school the next fall, reluctant but willing to use their toilets. He generally is at the point of doing a "really gotta go" dance before he will use them.

Any parent or caregiver of a child with autism has probably had similar experiences in potty training their child. It's my understanding that age seven is a fairly common age for most to claim complete success. A family therapist Matthew and I had seen many years previously had made a comment about young children who live in chaotic homes being constipated. She felt that many young children intentionally held their bowels, as it was one thing in their chaotic lives that they could control. I thought this was pretty far out on a limb, but for whatever reason it stuck in my head. A few years later, while I was working as an AODA counselor, I mentioned this theory to a doctor while we were discussing a young woman we shared as a client. He declared that it was a very foolish theory, that it was impossible for anyone to actually hold their bowels. I immediately thought of stories I had read of our nation's slaves having to hold their bowels when working in the fields. I didn't give his opinion as much credit as I did the original therapist who discussed this with me. I haven't given this constipation business a whole lot of thought since then, although I will admit to spending more time thinking about it than most. After going through the potty training business with Steven, I have wondered if children suffering autism may be so difficult to potty train because their little lives feel so out of control that elimination may be the one thing they feel they have any control over. I eventually asked one of Steven's doctors, who specializes in autism, about this theory, and she felt it absolutely had merit.

The fact that I am married to a wonderful man hasn't slipped past me. Once Steven was potty trained, Benjamin began looking forward to taking him in the semi for occasional trips. He saw this as an opportunity to give me a real break as well as a chance for him to be more involved with Steven on a day-to-day basis. Steven still needed a great deal of help in all other areas of his daily living skills. He needed complete help in getting dressed and continual prompts to feed himself. Benjamin was willing to take on the responsibility and take Steven in the semi with him. To his disappointment, he learned the insurance company wouldn't cover riders under the age of twelve.

When Steven was a baby and stayed with us, I cleaned the house before he arrived and made sure I had nothing pending so that I could devote all my attention on him for three or four days. During the two years I babysat for him and after he moved in, I found it very difficult to get my gardening and household chores done. I didn't know if it was so much his need for constant attention or his being used to having my undivided attention, but he was my constant companion. I was aware that he needed love and attention and found it difficult not to lavish him with love instead of doing chores. While I cooked or did dishes, he sat on the kitchen floor, rolling his balls against the walls. He sometimes played with cars that he could easily roll. He seemed to know the difference between necessary chores versus chores that could wait. He entertained himself while I did the necessary stuff, like fixing him something to eat, but when it came to me doing chores that could wait, he wanted me to spend time with him instead.

Steven liked to swing, and so we often went to the nearby children's park, where I pushed him for long periods of time. Children with autism like the swinging motion, which is believed to center and soothe them, especially when they're agitated. Not that Steven needed much soothing; he was a very contented little boy. An interesting little swinging incident happened on his fourth birthday, when he had been staying with me for several days. I was scheduled to take him back to his parents by noon for his birthday celebration. I decided that I would take him to the children's park and push him in the swing for as long as he wanted. We went early, and I was into my second hour of pushing that swing, thinking he would tire pretty soon. He never giggled or laughed, and I wasn't certain he was having fun until I held out my hands to help him out of the swing, then he'd cry. Although he was still nonverbal, he was making his desires known, so I pushed him some more. All of a sudden, he started laughing very loudly, and I thought, *How odd! Why would he start laughing, and so loudly all of a sudden when nothing had changed?* Then I saw two teenage boys walking toward the tennis courts. Steven was showing off, trying to get their attention, as if saying to them, "Look at me! I'm having so much fun!" He laughed and squealed in delight until they left the court, then he became somber and quiet again. Observing this behavior gave me a clearer insight into his need for recognition: he was here in this world. He mattered. I pushed Steven a bit longer after the teenagers left, and when it was time for us to go, he still didn't want to leave the swing.

Because he liked me pushing him in the swing, I bought a child's glider swing for his sixth birthday. I also bought galvanized pipe, the elbows, a bag of cement, and hardware to hang the swing, and I put the whole thing together myself and cemented it into the ground. *There!* I thought. *Now I'll get some gardening work done, and he can swing and watch me.* It didn't quite work out that way. If I didn't stand there and watch him swing, he just sat there. If I turned to look at him, he'd begin swinging. He was beginning to show a definite pattern of willingness to do things for himself, but only if someone was observing him.

Benjamin and I encouraged Steven to become more independent at home. Before he ever touched anything, he always looked at us, as if waiting for permission to touch it or to be told not to touch it. When Steven and I were outside and Benjamin was a few feet away in the garage, Steven waited for permission to walk into the garage. Because Steven liked swinging so much, I hoped this would be an activity he would pursue independently, so I purposely set his swing where I could easily supervise him from our screened-in porch. Sometimes I sat on the porch and watched him not swing, and I would call out to him, "You're not swinging. Let me see you swing. I'm watching you." When he took the initiative to move the swing back and forth a few times, I gave him lavish praise. "Wow!" I always said, "look at how good you can swing!" But he never swung independently, and he outgrew the swing by age nine. The galvanized frame was converted into a wonderful bird feeding station.

When Steven was seven, Benjamin and I installed a small basketball hoop on the garage wall so he could learn to bounce the ball on the concrete floor and practice coordination. He became quite the hoops shooter! He enjoyed shooting hoops and would play for hours if he had an audience, either Grandpa or me. There were, however, short periods of time that he would stay out in the garage and shoot hoops by himself. This was his very first step at any independence.

There is one thing Steven did without supervision, but it's something Benjamin and I kept very close tabs on and tried to limit. After our addition was complete, we set up a TV/VCR in Steven's play area so he could occasionally watch a child's video when we preferred to watch other programming. We used this to try to strengthen his independence, to teach him to be alone downstairs in his play area and trust that we were nearby. We introduced him to the concept of choices. He could select which video he wanted to watch. Watching videos was a touchy area with us, as we were aware that plopping Steven in front of the VCR was pretty much how he had spent his days when he lived Tina. There were times he would have preferred spending more time watching videos than we allowed. It was nice to see his independence and trust strengthening, and I will admit that the hour-long breaks were nice for me. It's amazing the chores that can be done in an hour's time, or how rested one can feel just being able to relax for that hour.

Because Steven was still so regressed, we engaged in activities to strengthen other skills. We live in a rural area, surrounded by forests. Steven had poor coordination so I purposely took him for walks in the woods over uneven, brush-covered ground. When we came to fallen trees, I had him walk along their trunks. I also set up walking planks at home so he could learn to balance. On our walks, we counted flowers, I told him what birds we were listening to, we touched pine needles and the leaves of other trees and plants, and we smelled the different smells of plants. We also watched clouds. Sometimes they moved fast, other times they formed shapes, which I asked him to name. We sat in the grass and touched it, and I found worms for him to hold, though he didn't care too much for the worms. We explored everything, and I was always looking for new textures and smells to introduce him to.

Steven continued rubbing the knuckles of anyone close to him. Whenever he sat in anyone's lap, or even while eating at the table, he tried to reach the nearest person to rub his or her hand. It was very annoying, especially at meals. We refused to let him rub our hands at the table, sometimes keeping our hands out of his view or reach. When Steven sat in Grandpa's lap and tried to rub his knuckles, Benjamin changed it to a hand holding game instead. By turning it into a game, within a few short weeks, Steven was climbing into Benjamin's lap with a mischievous grin, seeking to play a hand game rather than rub his knuckles. All the times we had told him no had had no effect, and now I was surprised that something Steven had done consistently from birth until he was seven years old had been easily discouraged and turned into a game. Steven hasn't forgotten the hand game. He still occasionally wants to play it with Grandpa.

Steven has an amazing memory. Meme lived in two different motels when she followed Matthew and Steven to our area. One has been torn down, but its old sign is still in place. Steven was four years old when he visited Meme in these two locations. Although he had never commented on it before, when he was nine and we were driving past these motels, he started announcing, "Meme used to live there." He even recognized the vacant lot.

He is such a pleasant little fellow. I was given many assurances that he was a popular student at school. He certainly was popular with the adults. Then, as now, he surprised most people he meets by remembering their names, and he can generally tell them where he last saw them. For instance, if we encountered someone in a certain store, he would comment that he had seen them there. With as many adults as one has contact with at any elementary school, this really is impressive.

While we were out walking one afternoon, I talked to Steven about writing his story. I told him that because it was his story, if there was something he'd like to make sure I included, he better tell me before I finish it. "I'll think about it," he said. At that time, when he talked about himself, he usually referred to himself as "he." "He'll think about it," would have been a more typical answer. Whenever he makes a more appropriate statement, I know he's on a roll and something good is going to happen. As we talked, I was quite aware that he could, and very possibly would, give me another glimpse into his spiritual wisdom. *It'll be something wonderful to conclude his story with*, I thought.

At lunch the next day, he clearly said, "Meme walked up to him and kicked him. She walked away, then came back and kicked him again. She couldn't find her necklace."

Those statements haunted me for the rest of the afternoon. Because of his incorrect pronoun usage, I didn't know if he was talking about himself or his dad. He has never talked about his life before he came to live with us and has never made innocent statements revealing his past, as children sometimes do. Nor have Benjamin or I ever tried extracting information from him. I didn't know if I could handle hearing about any of the abuse I suspected he'd endured.

When Steven and I were able to talk again later that day, I asked him if he was talking about himself or his dad when he talked about Meme kicking.

"Me!" he exclaimed, pounding his chest with his fist and tears welling in his eyes. "She kicked me!"

"Are you telling me this because I'm writing your story?" I asked him.

"Yes."

"Is this something you want me to write about in your story? Do you want me to put it in your book?"

"Yes!"

"Is there anything else you want me to write about?"

"Later," was all he said. He didn't want to talk about this stuff any more that day.

In the months following these revelations, I have periodically asked Steven if there was anything else he'd like me to "include in your book." It wasn't that I wanted grisly stories. I realized he remembers his abuse. He was carrying around a lot of pain and needed a safe place to dump it. Instead of worrying if I could handle hearing it, I decided it was more important that he be able to tell someone about it. But when I asked, he always responded, "Later." At one point I said, "Honey, it doesn't have to be bad stuff. You can talk about happy things, too." "It's all naughty," he said. There have been no other disclosures. I don't push the issue. One has to know Steven to appreciate his uniqueness. He seems to be quite aware of what his destiny is, and he is controlling much of its course.

While I was still doing "potty patrol" at school, I was disappointed when I saw what Steven's daily routine consisted of. I realized that most of what he had learned so far academically was what Benjamin and I had been teaching him at home. This is not to say he hadn't learned anything at school, but I wasn't sure I could determine Steven's ability to learn with the goals that were established for him on his IEP (Individual Educational Program).

Steven spent some of his day learning his ABC's. One teacher had him stringing beads and sewing on sewing cards, and I was impressed with her ability to get him to do such a coordinated activity. His speech therapist worked diligently and successfully to improve his use of words and to teach him new words. They also worked on blowing, sucking, and a variety of other tasks, but speech therapy was limited to two hours a week. Occupational therapy—needed to improve balance, hand coordination, and dressing skills—also worked with some success, but, again, it was limited to one or two hours a week. The fact that he was accomplishing goals in speech and occupational therapies in those limited hours made me believe he was capable of learning more academically, considering all the hours he was in school.

Because I was disappointed with what I thought were limited academics and low expectations of Steven, I discussed these issues with the school psychologist and asked that staff conduct a more rigorous program with him. After all, slowly but progressively, he was beginning to count and had learned a few colors in the limited amount of time that Benjamin and I had to teach him at home. That darned pleasantness and wonderful gentleness that characterizes Steven can be a real hindrance if he's allowed to manipulate people into not wanting to upset him. I was wondering if that was why they had low expectations for him at school.

This is not to say the school day went without Steven having crying spells. In his first two years in early childhood classes, when he was still living with Matthew, he worked through the challenge of experiencing people and activities in transition. It is common for children with autism to have difficulties with such changes. Each morning, when Daddy dropped him off at school, he began crying. Some days he cried when leaving school. If I visited their apartment, Steven cried when I left. Whenever there was a transition of people, Steven cried.

I remember Steven making another transition, leaving one classroom to walk all the way across the hall to his next classroom. The teacher had to stand in the doorway and assure him that he was okay, that he could cross the hall alone. The teacher he worked with next had to stand in her doorway and encourage him to keep coming. He was in first grade and into his second year living with us when he successfully completed this transition. Once this was accomplished, he was soon able to walk the halls to his next classroom, unassisted. The teacher he was leaving would call the expectant teacher to let her know Steven was on his way. Before long, he found his way easily around the school to all his classrooms, unassisted and without the phone calls.

When Steven was in first grade, his speech therapist sent home a note saying that he wanted to show us he could drink through a straw. He did it! This was something else that brought me to tears, and Benjamin and I celebrated his accomplishment by taking him out for supper. We ordered a big glass of soda that he could drink through the straw. He was so proud. As any parent knows, it is such a relief to have their child finally drink from an open cup or glass, as it means no more worrying about packing sippy cups or bottles every time they leave the house. We did that until Steven was seven, and what a relief it was when it was no longer an issue. Before Steven joined us, Benjamin and I had been quite spontaneous when it came to going places or eating out. But then there were several times, when we realized we didn't have a sippy cup with us, that we decided it would be easier to go home than to have a spontaneous meal in a restaurant. This drinking through a straw business gave us freedom most people can't imagine. To this day, I often think about how such a simple thing made such a difference, and I think wonderful thoughts about the hard, consistent work his speech therapist did to accomplish this.

Teaching Steven anything academic was difficult, either at home or at school. We have ten steps to the top of our deck, and from the time he began visiting, I counted each step with him to teach counting. He was almost eight years old and still would not participate. His ability to identify colors was limited to three or four colors. Over/under concepts seemed to elude him. Benjamin and I knew there were other learning disabilities besides the disabilities associated with autism, and we questioned Steven's capacity to learn. After two years of the structured and stable living conditions we provided for him, there had been less progress than we hoped for academically.

Because of Steven's slow academic progress, Benjamin and I decided to have him tested at the clinic where he had received neurological care for his infantile spasms. This was an effort on our part to better understand Steven's capacity to learn. Perhaps we could learn different approaches to strengthen his comprehension. Steven and I made several trips to the clinic to complete all the testing, and I am so blessed that he loves riding in the car because it was a seven-hour round trip. The clinic first tried to determine why Steven was learning disabled. They exhausted all tests looking for chemical or genetic imbalances that would explain his delays. They found nothing conclusive.

Children like Steven who suffered severe infantile spasms are generally mentally delayed after the spasms are controlled. This seems to be the best explanation for his delays. While suffering seizures, the brain shuts down at critical times when these babies would otherwise be learning. Steven's seizures lasted several months and were severe in intensity. His medical condition, along with Tina's refusal to include him in therapies that would have helped him after the seizures were controlled, contributed to his gross delays.

Steven's academic testing indicated that in many areas he was functioning at eighteen months, while in other areas he was functioning at about thirty-six months. This wasn't much for an almost eight-year-old boy, and it was heart-wrenching for me. This was after he had been with us for two years and had already made some noticeable progress.

The clinic recommended contacting a service that might be available to us. It provided personnel to work individually with children with autism in a home setting. Children with autism can be easily distracted by other activities in the classroom, so the individual attention they get working with home workers is a real advantage. There are several differences in the way the information is presented that also make a difference in the way these children are taught. Because of their short attention spans, the teaching program is structured with work for five minutes, then play for five minutes, gradually increasing the time for each. The teachers give the children loud applause, cheers, and recognition when they succeed. Benjamin and I knew that bringing this help into our home would be a major adjustment, as if we hadn't already overhauled our lives. Having therapists come into our home on an almost daily basis to work with Steven would mean an end to our private little world, but it also held the hope of opening up Steven's world.

Shortly after completing the testing at the clinic and getting the recommendation for in-home help, Steven and I went on another of our walks. He began crying, and when I asked what was wrong, he said, "I want to be like the other children." I talked to him about the many ways he was like other children and told him I would do everything possible to help him learn the things that other children understood. In my heart I thanked God that he had provided the very answer—the referral to the clinic—at exactly the time Steven was ready.

I believe that events happen in our lives and people enter our lives by God's design. I believe there are wisdom and emotional growth offered with every problem we encounter. But it is up to each person to recognize the lesson and derive something positive from each new experience, even the difficult experiences. Because of my belief, when disruptions happen in my life, I don't get too "crazed out." Benjamin and I were determined to do whatever it took to offer Steven his best chances at life. We knew we needed the extra help that in-home services would provide. But having so many people into our home was daunting for me to consider. It's not that I just like being alone; I *savor* it. That's why Benjamin and I have adjusted so well to his being an over-the-road semi driver: when he was away, I had time to myself. After two years, I still had my moments struggling with having Steven living with us.

The first prayer I learned as a child was a prayer to my Guardian Angels, and it went:

Angels of God, my guardians dear,
To whom God's love permits me here.
Ever this day be at my side
To light, to guard, to rule and to guide.

This has remained the most meaningful prayer for me. I have prayed to my angels for guidance from the time I was a little girl, and I believe they have indeed listened and guided me. I have never stopped praying listening for their guidance. Two years earlier, when Benjamin came home and informed me that he had decided we should raise Steven, my very first thought was a quick, frantic prayer to my angels for help. Now, feeling as if my life was about to be invaded with in-home workers, I found myself praying again to be able to cope. I also prayed for the patience I knew I would need. I knew it would be provided. I think that is the secret to praying: you have to believe your prayers will be heard and answered. The answers aren't always exactly what you hoped for, of course, but when we ask for guidance, we receive insights into how to resolve and/or cope with our problems. It's up to us to listen for the answers. It's up to us to do the work. That's life—working through our challenges. We don't ask for divine intervention to wave a magic wand and make everything unpleasant go away.

My complete belief in God having a plan for me has had its drawbacks, too. From time to time, it has prevented me from recognizing and/or acknowledging my feelings. There are times when I want to stamp my feet and scream and cry like a spoiled child. "Hey, God—this isn't fair! Why do I have to be doing this? This isn't what I wanted to do!" Intellectually, I haven't been able to let myself let loose and carry on like the child in me wants to. Spiritually, how can I be angry that my life is going just the way I believe it's supposed to be going? I don't always claim to understand why certain events are happening in my life, but I trust that by facing my challenges, my life will be enriched. I'm not a spiritual being; I strive for spirituality. I am a human being, struggling to deal with life as I live it.

And this human being is recently postmenopausal. Talk about a hormonal readjustment! While corresponding via e-mail with a friend, I had an insight. Our messages had to do with concerns over the troubled paths our adult children had taken. Rather than making definite, positive, healthy changes to make their paths a little more pleasant, they seemed to be stuck in futile patterns. During this correspondence, I realized that I felt that I had been ripped off of my menopausal years. Menopause happens when most women are looking at an empty nest. It is just the course of life. You raise your children, go through all the heartbreak and triumphs of those years, then they go away and leave you feeling empty and wondering what comes next. Then—*bam!* What's next is this marvelous, complete transformation of mind, body, and spirit. This is supposed to be a quiet time of a woman's life, when she can delve into her innermost thoughts, evaluate her life, search her soul, and adjust to the slowing down of her body.

When I was a young woman and my friends and co-workers were making their snotty, ill-informed observations of how dreary it must be to become old, I sought counsel from the older women in my life. I admired and respected them and their wisdom. Because they seemed so comfortable with themselves, I looked forward to aging. Writing to my friend now, it came crashing down on me that the quiet, introspective time of life that I had looked so forward to had, in fact, come and gone. I was darned angry about having missed it by being so busy raising my grandson. I wasn't mad at Steven. No, I was angry with Matthew, with his inability to care for Steven.

I felt intense anger, but then it was gone in a flash. I believe this was an insight presented to me at that moment by my guides. They wanted me to acknowledge that I was tired of being really mad at Tina and Matthew. Anger is so destructive, and I really didn't have time for it. It consumed too much energy that I would need elsewhere. It felt good, though, to have connected with my very human feelings of "poor me." That's why I am here on earth: to think and feel as a human being, then to strive for spirituality.

What is a successful life? To me, success lies in being content and happy. Living life with no regrets, being grateful for what we have, whether it's our health, financial security, or good friends. Whatever is important to each of us, overcoming the obstacles in our individual paths, that's what adds quality to our lives. At least that's what I believe.

I consider my recovery from the insanity of alcoholism—from having been raised in an alcoholic home and my own alcoholism—nothing short of a miracle. There was a time I saw life as hopeless and questioned whether life on earth wasn't, in fact, hell. But I slowly crawled up from that cesspool of hate, distrust, and suicidal behaviors. Recovery transformed every aspect of my life. I'm glad I'm alive. I'm glad I'm able to help Steven experience life in a way that is so different from what it would have been if Benjamin and I had not intervened.

I am also blessed to have such a loving companion, a man who is totally committed to improving Steven's life. I'm blessed that he and I are working together to teach this boy love, trust, and all the wonders of life. My shy, quiet husband not only opened his heart and home to Steven, but he also joined me in opening our private sanctuary so that people could enter and help Steven improve his academic and daily living skills. Together, Benjamin and I have accepted all the challenges and blessings of this God-sent opportunity.

# Chapter 6

## *A Candle for the Children*

When we had Steven tested so we would know what learning abilities we could anticipate or push him toward, it was rather daunting. The specialists determined that the most we could expect would be for Steven to achieve a first grade level of comprehension by the time he was an adolescent. The very best we could hope for would be a fourth grade level, but the doctor concluded by saying, "I would love nothing more than to be wrong with my prognosis." He added that he hoped we would return someday and that Steven would drive the car to the appointment. "There's always hope," he said.

The specialists had excellent recommendations for us. They suggested that Benjamin and I speak more slowly to Steven. By talking slower and using fewer words, Steven could have better comprehension of what we were saying to him. They also suggested that we play simple games with him. To teach him over/under concepts, we were to place a stuffed toy on a chair and tell him, "On the chair." We would then put the toy under the chair and say, "Under the chair." To keep this "homework" consistent with Steven's work at school, his speech therapist sent home a large laminated Valentine heart with instructions to place it first on top of a rug, then under the rug, then to ask him where the heart was. With repeated requests, he was to learn to respond, "The heart is on the rug," and, "The heart is under the rug." Keeping the work consistent with school was beneficial. It helped Steven learn that a given concept was the same at school and at home. The over/under games were expanded to "on the table," "under the table," and so on, until he grasped the concept in general. When traveling, Benjamin and I began to tell him, "We're going under the bridge," or "We're on the bridge, going over the river." We were able to see Steven learning to respond correctly when asked where objects were, but somehow comprehension still wasn't there. Through the years we have consistently instructed him on these concepts, and although there has been progress, we know we can't really expect him to understand the next time we tell him the toy he's looking for is "under the chair."

The specialists at the clinic told us there were several companies that offered in-home services for children with autism. This is due to the increasing number of children being diagnosed with autistic disabilities and also because it has been proven that early intervention enables many autistic children to mainstream into regular classrooms. I contacted the agency offering in-home services in our area and made an appointment for an evaluation. One worker interviewed me while another tested Steven's willingness to learn. Steven had just turned eight at this time, and generally eight years is the cutoff age for this agency to accept children for therapy. The services had not been available in our rural area until shortly before I was referred to them, and for that reason they accepted Steven even though he was just slightly over their age limit. The services were available to those who otherwise would have missed out on any help.

The woman who tested Steven found him to be an eager learner, and so their services were soon integrated into our lives. Of course, Benjamin and I continued working with Steven. It is important for families to reinforce the instruction the child is getting, rather than putting all expectations on in-home service staff. This is true with all children: the more their parents teach them, the more they will learn.

Because Steven was receiving SSI benefits for his disabilities, these services were paid by the Medical Assistance programs. "Thank goodness" is all I have to say for that. Benjamin and I would never have been able to afford all this in-home help. Although these therapeutic services are funded by taxes, we pay taxes, too, and we have tried to make conscientious decisions to ensure our tax money is spent wisely and that the agency's time with Steven was productive. We were thus involved in the lesson plans, and if the work seemed to be unproductive, we asked for changes. This was a three-year program of intense therapy, giving Steven twenty hours a week of hands-on tutoring. He was assigned a social worker, who was required to make a home visit every two months to evaluate the program and its progress.

Benjamin and I were so conscientious of how the health care money was being spent that I spoke to Steven's social worker about it. An incredible amount of public money is now being allocated to children with autism requiring in-home services. The social worker explained that most children are younger than Steven when professionals work with them, and obstacles are more easily overcome with younger children. By spending the money on younger children, public officials believe that the children may grow up to become functional, tax-paying adults who will put the money back into the system. Regardless of Steven's age, he was always referred to as the "poster child" of our county's Social Services, as he was doing exactly what the money was supposed to help him do.

In-home therapy is not intended to replace public or private school services for autistic children. It is in addition to the child's work at school. Children are evaluated to determine their willingness to learn and how long they are capable of working without becoming frustrated. Some children are scheduled to work at home for two hours, while others need to stay on task up to six hours. With Steven's twenty-hour allotment of in-home services, his schedule was mind-boggling. School days involved getting on the bus at 7:35 a.m. and arriving home at 3:50 p.m. Then we had to fit in twenty hours of instruction after school. Even three hours, five days a week is only fifteen hours, so he also spent Saturday mornings from 8:00 a.m. until noon with a tutor. Our Saturday mornings were set up this way so Steven would not be exhausted on school nights. It was also advantageous to keep the teaching flowing on a near-daily basis rather than having a two-day break. The agency referred to their personnel as "workers" and "counselors," but when I tried to explain the help we were getting, I always referred to the workers as "tutors." More people seemed to understand "tutors," and I had to answer fewer questions.

With a full day of school, plus the three hours of additional tutoring, it wasn't until seven o'clock at night that Steven's day ended. He was tired. He wanted to go to bed by 7:30. But such full days meant that Benjamin's and my actual hands-on time with our grandson was cut down to almost nothing at all. We believe that children need the bulk of their instruction in life skills from their families, but as Steven's guardians, it was difficult for us to have such limited time with him. I was so stressed out, in fact, that my hair began falling out by the handful. Although I had the freedom to leave home while the tutors were present, I preferred to stay so that when Steven was on his fifteen-minute outdoor break, I could spend that time with him.

We did whatever Steven wanted to do during his break time, whether it was playing kickball, shooting hoops, or going for walks. He may have thought he was taking a break, but all games and physical activity strengthened his coordination. He was learning how to play the games and share and take turns. Our walks were opportunities to teach him big/small concepts. The tutors and I picked different-sized flowers and stones and asked him which were big and which were small. We even compared the sizes of shadows to show him short and tall. We counted steps and felt the blacktop (teaching him hot in the sunshine and cool in shaded areas). To learn coordination, we kicked stones and pine cones and threw stones at utility poles, which strengthened his hand-eye coordination. There are many instructional activities for any child while out on walks, and Steven needed the instruction over and over. Besides wanting to spend break time with Steven, I also wanted to be home for those times when he did exceptionally good work, so he could run upstairs to show me what he did. If I heard excitement downstairs, I could go down to praise him and, yes, to observe and "snoopervise."

At church, the congregation prays the Lord's Prayer in unison, and because Steven wanted to participate in the Mass, he was very willing to learn this prayer. He was usually exhausted by bedtime, but he wanted to learn this prayer, so when he went to bed, I helped him to recite it. While his tutors struggled with his academic work, I helped him with the Lord's Prayer and after only a few evenings, he knew it. The same goes for a favorite book from that time, a story about children's family loving them forever, in case they ever wonder. Steven wanted me to read that book to him every night. It's thirty pages long. After two weeks, he picked it up and said he would read it to me. He had the words on each page memorized within a very short time. The fact that Steven can learn what he wants, when he wants, does create impatience and frustration in Benjamin and me when, despite repeated instructions, he seems to not understand or grasp the significance of other things we're trying to help him learn.

Until in-home services were arranged, Benjamin and I had been very private people. We never had many visitors. Before Steven moved in, I even used to do my yard work in the nude, and the only time I was ever interrupted was when a Jehovah's Witness came to convert me. I hid behind the corner of the house watching my clothes gently swaying in the breeze from the post I hung them on earlier. It seemed a long time before I heard the car pull out the driveway.

It was quite the change, therefore, to have at least one person a day, six days a week, in our home. It wasn't just one tutor, either. To forestall any child becoming too conditioned to one person's style of instruction, a variety of teaching styles and personalities are presented to the child, which means he meets more than one tutor. When new employees needed to be trained, the agency asked for our permission to have them train with tutors working with Steven, which meant that often there were two tutors. Senior counselors and/or a supervisor also came weekly to supervise the tutors' work and ensure that it was consistent and being presented in the correct format. Because we already had the entire lower level of our home set up as Steven's play space, it was easy enough to convert that into his tutoring space. Our lower level is built into a hill, with the front exposed and an outside door, making outdoor playtime or working activities easily accessible without anyone having to walk though the main home. Looking back on those three years of therapy for Steven, having that door helped enormously to alleviate my sense of being invaded.

One of the first things Benjamin and I wanted Steven to accomplish was feeding himself independently. It was very frustrating to have to tell him with every bite, "Scoop it up," then, "Take a bite." It was often necessary to tap his dish lightly to get his attention focused on the task of eating. Every day, every meal, for those first two years that Steven lived with us, it was "Take a drink," "Scoop it up," "Take a bite." If we didn't tell him, he just sat there! It befuddled me, as there were times when there was no way he could not be hungry. It seemed as though he had no basic instincts.

At mealtime, his tutor would sit with him at the table and help him while Benjamin and I ate in what was hoped might be a more relaxed fashion. The tutors were invited to eat with us, and, depending on their plans for the evening, sometimes they joined us. Other times, they just worked with Steven. Sometimes, however, Benjamin and I ate alone while the tutors worked with Steven. He learned to poke, scoop, and cut his food. We had previously kept most of his food cut very small or mashed that he could feed himself by scooping. With the continual tapping of his plate and encouragement to finish, he gradually became more able to complete the task set before him: eating.

We were also free to leave the house while a tutor was working with Steven, and so when Benjamin came home early enough, we sometimes went to a nearby restaurant for a Friday night fish fry. It was a rare, relaxing little break. Steven is a sensitive little guy, and he knew this eating business was a sore spot with us. He also knew Benjamin and I were going out to eat without him. I believe the fact that he knew he was being excluded from our occasional fish fries did more than anything else to encourage him to make some much-needed changes and learn to eat more independently.

At one point, I began getting a strong pulling at my gut that there was something very wrong at school. My guides made it loud and clear. They told me to schedule a tutor to go to school at lunch and work with Steven there, too.

From the beginning, we always worked hard at home to allow Steven to make choices. We taught him it was okay for him to have personal preferences. The tutor began her first day at school by helping Steven to choose his milk (strawberry, white, or chocolate). He chose chocolate. Trying to be helpful, the kitchen staff told the tutor that Judy, the aide most often assigned to Steven for lunch, said that Grandma doesn't want him drinking chocolate milk, so she always made him take white milk. Bless this tutor, who said, "Well, Grandma lets him drink chocolate milk at home, and if he wants chocolate milk today, he can have it." The tutor cleared it with me that it was okay if Steven chose chocolate milk. As the kitchen staff continued trying to be "helpful" to the tutors, it became apparent that Judy was denying Steven many foods simply because she always had to cut it up or help him to eat or prepare it in some way. Before the tutors were integrated into school lunchtime, Steven was actually getting a very limited menu. So much for good nutrition at school. There is evidence that the chocolate in milk prevents the body from absorbing calcium, so perhaps Judy was seeing to it that he did get some nutrients with the white milk.

It was not easy, nor was it the agency's wish, to use state-funded tutoring to overlap in a public school setting. As dedicated as any teacher may be, they are only as good as their aides, who are there to follow instructions given by the teacher. It was the middle of the school year when the tutors began working with Steven at school to keep the self-help skills he was learning at home consistent with mealtime at school. At school, as at home, the tutors worked with him to teach him to open his own milk carton, unwrap the straw, and insert it into the carton. They also had to show him how to cut into his food, as with a piece of cake. When the food wasn't sectioned or spread around the plate, Steven had to be taught how to dig into it.

Most of us can remember lunch recess. It was generally our favorite part of the school day. Steven loved recess, too, but Judy let him poke his way through lunch, which meant he didn't have time to go out for some fresh air. She wasn't going to stand out on the playground with him on cold, windy days if she didn't have to. We asked Steven's tutors to stay with Steven on the playground during lunch recess. Steven had to be taught to play, and the tutoring agency's policy is hands-on instruction rather than simply monitoring. I believe this was more successful than just standing there, watching. Steven learned to shoot hoops and play with the other children. He also seemed to enjoy standing on the edge of the playground and watch the other children. He laughed at their antics, but I also think the laughing was much like swinging at the park, a way for him to draw attention to himself.

In our part of the country, early spring generally means cold mornings with temperatures warming enough in the afternoons so that most children carry their jackets home from school. Hats, mittens, and boots were still necessary for recess time, as the snow hadn't completely melted yet. There were several days when Steven came home with his boots on the wrong feet. I could understand the end of the school day being rushed and this occasionally being overlooked, but it was happening so often that I felt it wasn't an oversight. About this time, another parent called me to report that when she went to school to pick her children up, she heard Judy screaming at Steven, "Put your coat on, *now!*" Okay, time to talk to the school psychologist.

Judy was being verbally abusive to Steven, and someone was allowing him, on a fairly consistent basis, to walk down the hall with his boots on the wrong feet. I asked the psychologist, "If I were to send Steven to school on a regular basis with his boots on the wrong feet, would the school think I didn't care about him?" I think the psychologist took my concerns sincerely. She admitted that other parents were raising similar concerns and believed that if this particular aide were to continue working, she needed to be placed with older students who would not be easily intimidated. She promised me that Judy would be transferred the next year. A few days later, the psychologist called to say she'd had a staff conference to talk not only about my concerns but those of other parents, too. She stated that she expected an improvement in staff-parent relations.

From that point on, Steven came home with his winter cap pulled on tight and his hood over that and snapped in place. He had his mittens on, and his jacket was zipped and buttoned. He was so bundled up that he looked like an infant. Because of his disability, he lacked the reasoning skills that told him he could take these things off if he was too warm. So he got off the bus each warm afternoon sweating profusely, his face flushed. I saw immediately that someone thought they were teaching me a lesson. After the third day, I realized it wasn't going to stop until I stopped sending warm clothes to school. I didn't tell the psychologist about this, however, because I knew I was dealing with someone who didn't take kindly to reprimands. The deliberate overdressing of a helpless child, knowing there could be severe health consequences to the child, told me this was someone playing a power game. Quite honestly, I was afraid of what she would dream up next to show me I'd better keep my mouth shut. Steven was her pawn. He would be the one suffering. Common sense tells us that if one player stops playing the game, there is no game to play. So I stopped playing Judy's game.

Steven and I still played kickball outside while waiting for the bus, but just before he got on the bus I confiscated the hat and mittens and usually the jacket. The school year would be ending soon, and I had been assured that the aide would be transferred to work with older children next year.

When the tutors started going to school at lunchtime, the Saturday sessions were discontinued. But Steven has never lacked meaningful instruction. Everything Benjamin and I do with him, we try to implement some kind of learning. When I hang the clothes out on the clothesline to dry, I have him touch the wet clothes to learn "wet," and then touch them again when they are dry and ready to come off the line. We always discuss clouds and sunshine, shadows, and whether it is windy or just breezy. I don't think most people realize that children with autism have a very difficult time understanding these various concepts. Autistic children don't understand size and proportion; they try to sit in their Tonka trucks or crawl into doll houses.

I sometimes catch myself feeling fatigued at having to retrain my brain. I have to think with these different concepts and communicate them to Steven. Health professionals tell us that as we age, the more we read, play word games such as crossword puzzles, and do other things to keep the brain active, the healthier our brains and overall quality of our life will be. That means Benjamin and I are the fortunate ones. Our brains are getting a real workout!

Benjamin is such a fun person, and he's so wonderful at teaching Steven. I build Steven balancing beams, whereas Benjamin asks Steven if he can walk down the crack in the road when they're out on a walk. I wish I had Benjamin's talent for simplicity and spontaneity. Steven likes shadows. One day, he, Benjamin, and I were walking hand in hand, with Steven in the middle. It was a sunny day, and Benjamin took out the camera and took a picture of the shadows we cast. It is such a cool picture. The shadow Steven is looking up at the shadow Benjamin, and the photo perfectly captures his admiration. I blew the picture up to an eight-by-ten and framed it to hang in Steven's room.

The additional tutoring Steven received has made all the difference for him. The tutors work with the "whole person," and instruction is not limited to any specific area. In addition to the academics, we have had help with dressing skills, personal hygiene, becoming independent, and phone use. Children with autism can easily learn the correct response being sought from them. However, the primary goal is not just to extract the correct words; it is to help the child comprehend what the words mean. Steven worked with picture cards that show, for example, the word "cut" with a picture of a boy cutting a sandwich. These children have to learn the word association, and they seem to do it best with pictures. There's a lot of picture association at school, and Steven's daily schedule was composed of pictures that illustrated the planned activities for that day. He advanced so well with his reading skills that the school was able to eliminate the pictures, and Steven now has a written daily schedule. Watching him make this progress gives me goose bumps.

Benjamin and I have a saying: "It's all about Steven." We say it lovingly and jokingly. Yes, our lives revolve around Steven. We compromise and improvise and make all decisions in Steven's best interests. I am now past the resentments I felt earlier at my son and Steven's mother, but it dawned on me one day that it had been a long time since Benjamin needed to address his own confusion about how Steven's parents could be so irresponsible. I mentioned this to him, and he said, "I'm past that, too. I don't think about it anymore." We occasionally mention the fact that our lives would be enormously different without Steven, and we take a few moments to savor what it might be like to have a more carefree life. Then we get back to the business at hand. It's comforting to know that your partner is right there with you, all the way. We are equally committed in improving the quality of life for this very happy, open-faced, little boy. I often ask myself, "Am I blessed, or what?"

We went through the first year of intense therapy when Steven was in the second grade. When he came home from school, his tutor was here, ready to help him off the bus and bring him into the house to begin work. It was hard to see my grandson putting in those long hours, but, amazingly enough, he was pushing himself to learn. I was concerned that he should get more fresh air, so I cut a running loop with the lawn mower that measured one-tenth of a mile in a small field adjoining our backyard. I insisted that we either run or walk it every afternoon when he got off the bus before going in the house to work. When Steven first came to live with us, no matter how many times I tried to get him to run, he would run for four steps, then stop. With the loop, I'd say, "Go run the loop!" and he took off running. There were several days he ran four loops, nonstop. How could anyone expect any child to learn with that much pent-up energy? In the winter, we used the snowmobile to keep the loop packed down so he would be able to use it all year long.

I also bought another swing, a big-boy swing now, and securely installed it between two pine trees. If we are outside watching him, Steven will swing, but he won't swing on his own. Several tutoring hours had been spent both at home and at school to teach him to pump the swing himself. I wanted his breaks to be taken outside, weather permitting. In fact, any work that could be done outside, I wanted done outside. Swinging was as therapeutic as reading. It helped strengthen his coordination. I think it was time well spent. I have a hard time comprehending how anyone cannot figure out how to swing, and yet I am aware of the effort and time it took Steven to learn. The tutors, Benjamin, and I all took turns, first standing in front of Steven after we got him swinging, then pushing his feet down while saying, "Pump!" We did this for months before he dropped his feet on his own rather than holding them straight out in front of him. When Steven began dropping his own feet, we stood in front of him and dared him to touch us with his feet.

Summer was easier. The tutors still came five days a week, but it was morning hours, only four hours a day. We decided we could keep to five days a week because Benjamin and I weren't going to let Steven slough off on the weekends. Morning hours left afternoons for swimming and other activities, but even though we had afternoons off, we still felt restricted because we had to stay home all week so Steven wouldn't miss any sessions. That meant no trips out of town to visit friends or family. Occasionally, when there was an agency meeting that all the workers had to attend, Steven got a day off. On those days, we shot out of town for a quick, short break.

When third grade began, my hair started falling out again, big time. We were back to those long, late school days. I hated seeing Steven put in such long days. He had so little time to be a kid, carefree and just having fun. I soon found myself cracking the whip to "Keep the kid outside!" when he first got home from school. And at school, Judy in fact was not transferred to work with older children; she was Steven's primary aide again.

I don't always make decisions or changes that need to be made until I'm pushed. This is a flaw of mine. Now I was upset about Steven's long days and very upset that Judy would be having so much contact with him on a daily basis at school again. But I took no action, except what I could control at home. The tutors were still scheduled for lunch and recess at school. Although I didn't discuss my concerns about Judy with them, I knew they had Steven's best interests at heart and believed that if they noticed anything questionable at school they would bring it to my attention. I felt I would get a truer picture of events this way than if I set them up to watch for inappropriate behaviors.

Here is the short version of a very long story about what happened next. Steven's class had an opportunity to go to the YMCA for swimming classes. The school wanted to know if I would be willing to go to the Y and work with Steven in the water. Judy said she'd go and let Steven splash and play in the water, but that she was not going to get in the water. By this time I was getting pretty tired of hearing what Judy was and was not willing to do. If the truth be known, all I had to hear was that Judy would be attending Steven during his swimming lessons. It wouldn't have mattered to me whether she'd be getting in the water with him or not. I simply would have volunteered. As far as I'm concerned, Steven, Judy, and water just don't mix. It's as volatile as water and electricity. So I joined Steven for his swimming lessons each week at the Y.

This whole issue made me so angry, though, that I swore that the school could keep Judy, and I would keep Steven at home. I knew he was getting sufficient academic instruction from his tutors. What I had to do was fill out papers for the state for requirements for homeschooling. The tutoring agency, however, is not considered an alternative for homeschooling. I knew that. Nevertheless, it was very exciting to think that Benjamin and I would now have the opportunity to be more involved in Steven's instruction. Benjamin and I discussed homeschooling. He felt it was a bad idea. I pulled my weight on this one, though. By the time Benjamin and I were through hashing it out, I wasn't basing my decision on the anger I'd originally felt. It was just that the more we talked about it, the more sense it made to me that this change would have several advantages.

Then I met with the school psychologist to tell her my decision to home school my grandson. Of course, she was against pulling Steven out of school. Because Benjamin was also against it, I compromised. Steven loves going to school, and because "It's always about Steven," I said I'd allow him to go half days. He could ride the bus home at lunchtime when the bus brought the early childhood children home. I told the psychologist the school was on notice, however, that I might still pull him completely. Half days were to begin the week after Thanksgiving vacation, two weeks away, and that meant Steven would miss three swimming lessons, which would conclude after vacation. (I took him swimming at the Holiday Inn Express to make up for those missed sessions at the YMCA.)

Having made my decision, even though the change was two weeks away, I immediately began sleeping better at night and felt somewhat rested in the morning. My hair also stopped falling out, and there was a definite improvement in my blood pressure.

Steven's teachers at school were upset by my decision, and the first parent-teacher conference after he changed to half days was a little tense. However, after that first conference, they were very generous in agreeing that I had made a good decision on Steven's behalf. They were already seeing definite improvements in his overall life. Even Benjamin had to agree.

Obviously, the tutors were no longer needed at school for lunch and recess, and Steven began four-hour workdays at home. The tutoring was conducted in the afternoons, which proved to be much more effective. Not being so tired, he was better able to retain what he was learning. The tutor who worked Wednesday evenings had to continue at night, as she had a day job, but this was fine with me. Wednesday afternoons became Steven's and my outside play day.

Times change, of course, and tutors change, and progress is made, and summer rolled around again. That summer Steven had a wonderful opportunity to attend a camp with other autistic children. Camp was limited to children aged from eight to fifteen years old. It was a six-day camp; Sunday being registration day, and Friday afternoon completed the adventure. There were two counselors in each cabin of four campers. The children were given wonderful opportunities to fish, swim, kayak, go boating, roast marshmallows at the campfires and eat S'mores. There were arts and crafts, hiking, talent contests, yoga, and many more adventures for the children to experience. Most importantly, the children had fun with other kids just like themselves, and they left camp having made friends. Steven is a social little guy and did well with going to camp and being away from home.

The first year Steven went to camp was his fourth year of living with us, and Benjamin also wanted us to have a real family vacation. The week after camp, therefore, we took a week's vacation with Steven and traveled in the motor home to Lake Superior, where Steven was able to stand in the lake and let the waves crash in on him. He loved it. I did, too. The water was warm, something uncommon for Lake Superior, and very relaxing. We had a wonderful week of lakes, waterfalls, and Fourth of July fireworks. But then Steven wanted to go home. Two weeks is too long for Steven to be away from home, even when he's with us. We've learned to give him at least a few days at home between camp and our vacation week. On the downside of our adventures, I've noticed that he goes through a period of regression after his vacations. He acts helpless and unsure of himself, quite the opposite of what I expect.

The summer came to an end, Steven entered fourth grade, and we were into the third and final year of his intensive home therapy. Steven was still spending half days at school, which meant, of course, that I also had very limited time to attend to any business I had outside of home. I needed to be home at noon to get Steven off the bus and have lunch ready for him.

That fall, I sank into a horrible, deep depression, something unfamiliar to me. It was the first true depression I had experienced since my recovery from alcoholism, more than thirty years earlier. I lost my cool with Steven and was so ashamed that I found it difficult to forgive myself.

For months, Steven had been dressing himself completely and correctly. This was after two years of showing him his socks. "The gray goes on the bottom," I'd say as I slipped the socks on his feet. The next two years, I guided him hand-over-hand. During the fourth year, I only needed to supervise as he put his socks on himself. The same with the pants: "The zipper goes in the front." Shirts were the easiest, as occupational therapy at school and the tutors were also teaching him about shirts and buttons. The first appointment we had at the clinic for Steven's academic evaluation was the first day he put on his shirt by himself, and that was after two years of instruction at school and at home.

I was running late one morning. After those many months of correctly dressing himself as I only watched, I took the opportunity to put something away while he was getting dressed. When I returned to his room, he had his pants on backward and the gray padded soles of the socks were on the tops of his feet. I tried to contain my anger I felt and tried to squelch the quick, deeper breaths I take when I'm angry. With Steven's echolalia, I knew it would be a matter of seconds before he'd be mimicking my breathing. But I couldn't do it. He noticed my quickened breathing. He started copying me. "*Stop it!*" I hissed at him. "Now you're even trying to suck the breath out of me!" At least, I think I hissed it at him. I may have screamed. I don't know. My behavior that morning bordered on abuse, and this was before I realized that he remembered his past abuse. I only suspected that he understood he'd suffered terrible mistreatment. I still didn't want to even try to imagine what he might remember. There I was, disgusted with myself for becoming so angry and snapping at him. I went into such a deep depression that I found it difficult to talk. I was down to grunting to let people know, "I heard you, already." I stopped counting the steps when we walked up to the deck on our house. Steven started counting them for me.

In the following months while Steven was at school in the morning, I went for long walks. Walking allows me to clear my head and get into greater contact with my guides. I prayed for guidance. I prayed to help Steven overcome whatever abuse he had suffered. I prayed for forgiveness for being abusive to him. I prayed to get out of my funk, to get on with my life. I didn't want to die or have suicidal thoughts, but I did want to curl up and sleep for a very, very long time. My guides finally assured me that Steven was dealing with his old abuse issues and working his way through them. I needed to be there for him as I had been, and there wasn't anything more I needed to do.

It took time, but my depression gradually lifted. I concluded that it had settled in so deep because I wasn't taking time to process my feelings. I was feeling overwhelmed by everything that needed to be done with and for Steven. All the people coming into our home, nearly every day, and for so many hours had me stressed out, and I still had to deal with them on a daily basis. I couldn't even work through my depression in private! Steven's resistance to doing for himself what he could obviously do was just so frustrating for me.

Having had his grandma snap at him, Steven, being the sensitive boy that he is, apparently decided to knock off the nonsense about dressing. Since then, he has been correctly putting his socks on each morning, though he occasionally still puts his pants on backward. I no longer supervise his dressing. Each morning, he calls my attention to the fact that he is dressing correctly. Slowly, ever so slowly, things are getting better. Within days of my losing my cool, Grandpa also got upset with Steven about his pretending to be helpless when putting on and taking off his jacket. Steven decided that he can put on his jacket, hat, and mittens by himself. Just as in dressing each morning, each time he takes off his jacket, he points out to us that he did it correctly, not bunching his sleeves up into it. Getting those gloves and mittens on is no small matter, and he is also very careful about taking them off without bunching the fingers up.

Putting his gloves on is one of the dressing skills that the tutors helped Steven master. He had difficulty putting his bike gloves on before riding his bike, and those gloves have only partial fingers, just up to the first knuckle. The tutors used clear surgical-type gloves that he could see through, and with a lot of work (in a relatively short period of time compared to similar tasks) he mastered putting gloves on.

Steven is almost independent in brushing his teeth. Benjamin and I and the occupational therapists at school also worked with him to accomplish this. Of course, now he wants to walk around the house brushing his teeth and showing us he can do it. He still refuses to squeeze the toothpaste onto the brush, however, and needs help doing that.

Even with all of Steven's accomplishments, he is not completely independent in anything. He always leaves one small step in place, refusing to take it. It seems to me he's afraid that if he doesn't need us to help him, there will be no reason for him to live with us. He can, for example, unroll the toilet tissue and bunch it up correctly, but won't try to tear it off the roll. He needs Benjamin or me to do that. He then wipes himself. He will also sit quietly on the toilet, refusing to let us know when he is done or that he needs help. Good old tough love does not work with Steven. We occasionally let him sit longer than necessary, but to let him sit until he asks for help would be abuse. He'd sit until his legs turned blue from lack of blood flow. Steven gives me dirty looks at the table when his milk glass is empty. With all his success at eating independently, he refuses to say, "May I have more milk, please?" For three years, we've tutored him and given him every conceivable prompt. Including pouring milk into small pitchers from which he can refill his own glass, yet he still expects me to know when he needs more milk. Everyone has to guess if Steven would like something to drink, even on hot days. Tough love doesn't work here either; he'd become dehydrated. Benjamin installed Steven-friendly water faucet handles on the bathroom sink. With these levered handles, he can independently pour himself water when he gets thirsty, but he doesn't really like water. He did, however, learn to use getting a drink of water as an excuse to take a break from tutoring!

Steven had been taking recyclables out to the proper containers for over a year, but he occasionally acts crippled if Benjamin asks him to do something that involves opening the door. This nonsense with Grandpa is, of course, another way to get his undivided attention. But it doesn't make sense to us, as our attention is always focused on him. I understand this behavior from children in negligent homes, because even negative attention is better than no attention, but this shouldn't be the case with Steven. Benjamin replaced our door knobs with handles so Steven can open and close the doors by himself.

Steven has been consistent in demanding that our attention be focused on him. This hasn't been all bad. From the time he moved in with us, he has planted treasures in our hearts, and we only had to be carefully listening. He was so tiny and small as a six-year-old. He looked almost malnourished, and his treasures often came out tiny and small, to be granted only if we had an open ear tuned in to him. His coherent moments are priceless. We were leaving the city park after taking him to his first Fourth of July fireworks, for example, when from the backseat of the car we heard, "I love you, Grandpa. I love you, Grandma." And there was so much love in his voice. Or the times when we're riding in the car and he blurts out, "I'm very happy!" This we know is from his heart, because he still usually refers to himself as "he." "He's very happy," is what we usually hear.

Although having the help of the tutoring services made all the difference for Steven, we looked forward to its conclusion, shortly after school ended the year Steven was in fourth grade. Even the dogs seemed to be tired of the constant flow of people. Our Springer spaniels, Missy and Albert, were getting old, and I think they would have liked things quieter around the house. Scooby, our Brittney, had passed on several years ago. Any dog lover will tell you that their dogs have a way of communicating. Our dogs had been accustomed to my undivided attention, except for those days when I brought Steven home for his visits when he was a baby. Missy's demeanor announced her feelings: "Oh, it's that creepy kid again," whereas Prince Albert was more curious. He always sat by Steven's playpen, sled, or swing as his protector.

After Steven moved in, however, the dogs avoided him, and he didn't show much interest in them. That changed a lot during the year Steven was ten, along with his growing independence. When Steven finished his work with the tutors in the afternoon, he wanted to take the dogs outside and play with them. Because the dogs were older, they didn't run much, but wherever they went, Steven walked with them. I needed to keep an eye on Missy, though. I think there were times she wanted to take him into the forest and lose him there. She seemed to be thinking, "If the kid is gone, maybe all the other people will stay away too, and things will get quiet around here."

Prince Albert, however, found a way to make his displeasure regarding all the people known. Despite all the surrounding forests in which the dogs always discreetly eliminated, Prince Albert began using the very path that the tutors used to do his duty. That added to my list of things to do. Every day, I had to scoop his job up before the tutors arrived. On the occasional days I forgot or just didn't have time to get to it, they stepped in it. My theory that Albert was "laying out the welcome mat" for them had a few tutors taking it personally. I think Prince Albert *was* making a statement. He stopped using the path when the constant flow of people diminished.

Benjamin and I had a big graduation party for Steven when he completed his in-home services. In fact, we pushed his completion ahead by three months. Steven had met all the criteria that we and the agency had determined would be our goals. Prolonging his involvement would have only been completing the three-year time allotment, and he was becoming bored and noncompliant. Benjamin and I were eagerly looking forward to a normal summer and a normal vacation from school.

The first summer Steven was with us, Benjamin and I didn't know what to do to celebrate his birthday when he turned seven. We didn't know many neighbors, and few of them had children. I met one boy in his school who also had autism, although he was a few years older than Steven. I called his mother and invited her and her son to see the movie *Finding Nemo* as a way to make the day special. The mother thought it was a wonderful idea, but her son politely said, "No, thank you." I sat on our front deck crying. "What are we ever going to do?" I asked Benjamin. "We don't know anyone with kids. How are we ever going to celebrate his birthdays if we can't even convince one kid to join us for what I thought would be a fun day?"

What a difference five years makes in making friends with families with children. Steven plays well with children aged four to six, and so we had a yard filled with children for his graduation party. Some members of our church also stopped in to congratulate him, and others who had gotten to know Steven drove many miles to share his special day. He knew it was his party. There wasn't any confusion in his mind as to why all these people were here, and I was proud of him because he was very gracious to everyone who came to his party. A friend loaned Steven a graduation cap and gown to wear when the agency's director presented him with a certificate of completion.

Would Benjamin and I do the three-year program again, knowing what we were headed for and all the compromises we'd have to make? Absolutely! Steven can read now. He is reading second and third grade level books. I have teacher's editions of the old Dick and Jane books. The first time Steven read one of those stories, he read with the questions and exclamations in his voice at the appropriate places. Steven still likes to be read to, and we take turns reading other books together. He reads one page, and I read the next. Although he doesn't like to color, he will color pictures, and stay within the lines. One time at school he innocently looked up at the teachers as he continued scribbling big lines through the page and said, "Grandma will be so disappointed."

Steven can count to one hundred. He reads road signs and is able to say what specialty stores sell—autos, furniture, gas stations, groceries, etc. He knows the worth of coins and dollars, although he has no comprehension of monetary value. He can cut paper with scissors, stack blocks, and sort by color, size, and shape. He is self-confident. I appreciate all the teachers in his public school and know they worked hard with him, but they would never have been able to accomplish what the in-home services did.

I realize that Steven's accomplishments don't sound like much for an eleven-year-old boy. There are times I need to remind myself that as an eight-year-old he tested out at eighteen to thirty-six months. The progress he has made is indicative of his determination to overcome what he knows are his obstacles. When I was preparing for his graduation party, I looked through all the letters I received from the clinic regarding his evaluations. In one, there was a reference from one of the doctors: "Steven was one of the more fortunate ones having suffered infantile spasms." But there's nothing in the letter indicating why she felt he was "fortunate." That comment has always stuck in the back of my mind, and because I always have to have an explanation for things that make me feel uncomfortable, I thought a good time to get an answer would be before Steven graduated. I wrote to the clinic and asked them to explain why Steven was considered "fortunate." They answered that many babies who suffer the intensity and duration of spasms that Steven suffered never walk or talk.

Regardless of Steven's past difficulties, he still provokes great fluctuation in Benjamin's and my patience and acceptance. We still don't know what we can expect of him in terms of self-reliance. His tenacious unwillingness to become independent in any given self-help skills can be infuriating. When we asked Steven if he would ask his teachers for help to use the bathroom, and he said, "No," he meant it. When he got good and ready, he finally said yes and asked for help. Using the school bathroom is just one example of the many things Steven has declined to do. When he finally says yes to something, we know we can count on him to do what we are asking.

That is why his "later" response regarding his childhood abuse still has me emotionally wired. He has given no other examples of the abuse he has suffered, which he promised to reveal "later." He knows exactly what happened to him, and he will talk about it when he is good and ready. He has an understanding of himself and his path in life. He is moving along a definite course in his life, and it seems nothing will make him deviate from it. I believe we all choose the obstacles we want to work through in our life experience on earth before we are born. I believe we are born into families and encounter people along the way who enable us to fulfill our destinies. Once we begin living our lives and facing our obstacles, I think some people lose their spiritual connection and succumb to their obstacles. I don't want to believe that any child agreed to be born into a life of horrors and abuse, but if I believe what I do, then I have to accept that some actually agreed to it. It would be an easy cop-out for someone to read my thoughts and conclude that there's no reason to make any changes, that their kids knew what they were getting into before they were born. Absolutely not! I think they agreed to endure hardships to give others the opportunity to become better parents.

Steven has the wit and sense of humor of an old man. The year he moved in with us, we tried to teach him to say "Christmas." We would say, "Say Christ-," and he'd say, "Christ-." Then we would say, "Say -mas," and he would say, "-mas." Then we put it together. "Say Christmas," and he'd say, "Christ-Christ," and laugh at his joke. This went on for months. He never said Christmas. I tried tricking him. "I heard you talking in your sleep last night, and guess what you said? Christmas. So I know you can say it. Because I heard you." He just laughed and said, "Christ-Christ."

On Christmas Day, Benjamin, Steven, and I had to travel for several hours, and we sang along to Christmas carols on the car radio. During a news break, we turned the radio off, and it was quiet in the car. Ever so softly, we heard from the backseat, "Jeez, Grandma. He knows how to say Christmas." Benjamin and I were confounded by Steven's ability to hang onto that joke for so many months. Initially, we wondered if he understood the significance of giving us the gift of the correct pronunciation on Christmas Day. After getting to know him better and having him pull similar tricks, there is no doubt in our minds that he knew exactly what he was doing.

If Benjamin and I weren't so amazed and intrigued by Steven's spirituality, we'd probably be spooked by it. During Sunday worship, Pastor Sarafin once suggested that for one month congregants light a candle before each meal. When lighting the candle, they would say a prayer for the children of the world. On the ride home, I asked Steven if he would like to light a candle and say a prayer for children.

"Yes," he said.

"Okay. What should we pray for?"

"That they find happy homes. Like I did."

"Oh, okay. Why? Do you remember feeling lonely and afraid?"

"Yes."

I wish he had said more than just, "Yes," and I wish I could write more, but this is as good as a conversation with Steven ever gets.

For every meal thereafter, including lunch when Steven came home from school, we lit a candle and prayed that other unhappy children would find happy homes. Three meals a day. We were still lighting the candle long after the month was over, and I mentioned this to Pastor Sarafin before service one

Sunday. During the service, she asked Steven to stand beside her and tell the congregation about his candle. With her help, he explained he prayed that other children would find happy homes as he had. The congregation was very quiet after he spoke. Apparently that wasn't the response Steven thought he should get, as he then stated very defiantly, "Hey! I remember being scared when I was a little kid!" We are still lighting the candle before each meal, and I expect we always will. It has become a tradition.

Our mealtime tradition of lighting the candle and praying for children living in unhappy homes somehow evolved into Steven insisting that his story be told. Not only do I receive inspiration and guidance from my guardian angels, but there are also occasions when Steven's angels move into my territory and help me out with him. I know when they're his angels and not mine; their presence feels very different. Steven's angels have been with me as I've written his story, and I am honored to have been chosen to participate in his mission to help other children who live in unhappy homes. Benjamin, Steven, and I believe in the power of prayer, and we believe lighting candles and praying has results. Perhaps lighting candles is causing some adults to feel a nagging in their conscience to treat their children better. Hopefully, telling Steven's story will give other adults insights into their children's dilemmas and help them find new approaches for interacting with them.

Quite honestly, I don't know what results to hope for. Spiritually, I have been encouraged to believe that it's God's will, not mine, and that I have only been a tool used to compile the information required to strengthen Steven's prayer. I admit that I have doubts that praying alone will lead to sufficient changes in the unfortunate living situations Steven hopes to diminish. I don't think my doubts are an indication of faltering faith; rather, I feel that when one prays, it should be expected that it will take continued work and effort to accomplish whatever is being prayed for. Sure, I believe in miracles and divine intervention. I also believe in being realistic.

On almost any given day, I am made aware of another living situation no child should have to endure. The pain of suffering children often becomes almost more than I can bear, and I end up feeling overwhelmed by grief and inadequacy. I cannot make a difference. That's when I have to remind myself that Steven's prayer and this book will be calling in the troops to help. Those who will wish to help Steven will all have their own unique ways of making a difference. Understandably, some will be limited to what they feel are only small acts, such as praying, but we believe that each prayer will multiply and strengthen Steven's prayer, many times over. Perhaps some will do as Steven does: light a candle at each meal and say a prayer.

There are movers and there are shakers. There are organizers and planners, leaders and followers. Most of my friends seem to be activists, like leaders, movers, and organizers. I consider myself to be a "seed planter" and believe that very small acts of kindness (seeds) can grow into very big trees of kindness. Direct eye contact and a warm smile from a stranger have brightened many gloomy days for me, and I have noticed others also stand a bit taller when I give that smile away.

Like adults, children know right from wrong. I remember with embarrassment the hand gestures and the "that's okay, you don't have to explain" comments I used to get when people were dismissing my inappropriate behaviors or comments. They understood I was ill-bred. I also remember feeling dignity and pride when I conscientiously worked on changing my behavior after people told me, "Your behavior is not very flattering to you," or "Why would you want to say those sorts of things? It's very unbecoming, and those comments make you sound illiterate." I was being offered a choice. I was doing the damage to myself with my self-destructive behavior. No one was making me behave that way. I am so grateful to those people who didn't dismiss me with pity because of my upbringing but demanded more of me because they knew I had it in me to make a better life for myself than what I'd been taught. I wasn't being scolded, nor was I being reprimanded; I was simply being told my behavior was inappropriate. Seeds were being planted for me to grow on.

I regret dismissing Tina and her inappropriate behaviors and comments. Perhaps I could have been a bit more helpful to her if I had not overlooked what I didn't like seeing. I've asked myself what more I can do to strengthen Steven's prayer. I have decided to "plant more seeds." It's what I am good at. It's a strength I have, to be able to lovingly confront without crushing or damaging another's ego. But I have been lax in using my skills. I will also continue to pray and ask for guidance and direction. I will be courageous in facing new challenges when they present themselves. I ask God to always walk with me.

# Chapter 7

## *Some Final Thoughts*

When Tina and Matthew rode off into the sunset after the guardianship hearing, their happiness-ever-after lasted all of three days, though they continued living together for another stormy year before Matthew was able to make a complete break from her. I think that not having Steven connecting them anymore contributed to the end of their relationship. My own relationship with Tina and Meme continued with its usual ups and downs, but over time we seem to have to come to a better understanding of each other.

Meme never abused her monthly phone call restriction, and Tina also regulated her calls. Within a year, rather than making a monthly call, they called only on holidays. The next year, three and four months would go by before we heard from either Meme or Tina. As I write this, Steven has been with us for almost six years, and Tina is down to one or two calls a year. Meme has continued to call two or three times a year and requests visits about twice a year.

Meme never called again while intoxicated. She has been equally respectful in being sober when she visits Steven. While it isn't always the three months of sobriety that I demanded, her sobriety is always close enough that her nastiness is absent. Steven and I meet her at nearby parks for visits. Early on, Tina came with her. Meme has been honest and not trying to hide the fact that she is struggling and her only periods of sobriety are the few months previous to Steven's visits. My main concern, of course, has always been that Steven no longer be exposed to her drunkenness. She has apologized for her drunken behavior and the rudeness directed at me. (I know how difficult it is to make those sorts of apologies.) She has, in fact, even complimented me regarding Steven's improvements. She says she is happy now that Steven is living with us and that we are taking such good care of him.

During the first year Steven lived with us, Meme met a man named Paul, and they married after a brief courtship. They lived in a town about seventy-five miles from us, so when they wanted visits, they were the ones who drove to our town. I made one exception when Meme and Paul invited Steven and me to their second wedding anniversary, which was an outdoor campfire party. It was a nice visit, and Steven had a lot of fun playing with other children invited to the party. During the months following the party, Tina, who lived in the same town as Meme and Paul, called a few times, wanting to know when I was going to bring Steven down for another visit. She apparently thought that because I had driven down for the anniversary party, I was going to continue bringing Steven for visits at her convenience. She complained about her rights and accused me of being stingy with the visits. I wrote her a letter, which she could read several times and get a clearer understanding of my position, and reminded her that she had wanted to give Steven to Social Services and have him placed for adoption. Had she been successful, she wouldn't know where Steven was, much less be expecting visits. In the letter, I told her Steven would be singing solo three stanzas of "Silent Night" for Christmas Eve Mass and invited her, Meme, and Paul to come to church for his performance. They could visit him after Mass, and we could exchange gifts. They were a no-show. When we got home, there was a very inebriated phone message from Tina saying that her ride hadn't shown up and how sorry she was. I knew then that she had not extended my invitation to Meme and Paul. I'm sure they would have attended Mass just to see Steven perform.

After they missed the Christmas Mass, it wasn't until March of the next year that they called and asked to visit so they could give Steven his Christmas presents. Pastor Sarafin gave us permission to visit at the church on a Sunday afternoon. Tina was inebriated, but apparently not high enough, because she went out to the van "to get something" and came back even higher. Meme told me that Tina had been mouthing off during the trip, saying she was making plans to take me to court and take Steven away from me.

Steven has always been fairly unemotional after seeing his mother and grandmother. As we get into the car to leave, he looks a little teary eyed, but as soon as we pull away, he springs back to his happy self. He never talks or asks about his mother, though he will sometimes say, "Wait until Meme sees this!" when he successfully accomplishes something. He knows it will be something new for her to see.

Tina has always asked for overnight visits with Steven, and Meme also began suggesting that maybe he could spend an overnighter with her and Paul. As little as Tina and Meme see Steven, however, and after visiting for only an hour, they always begin arguing about who is going to take him to the bathroom this time, or it's, "You go push him on the swing, I'm tired." Their interactions with him are clumsy and awkward, and none of their visits have lasted more than two hours, as either Paul or Meme begins complaining of back pain or other ailments and they soon say their good-byes. What I wonder is how could Tina or Meme think they have the physical energy to have Steven for an overnighter when an hour with him wears them out?

Meme's and Paul's marriage has been rocky, in part because of her relapses. Tina has been a hindrance as well. During the fourth year of their marriage, Paul made Meme choose either him or Tina. Meme chose him, at least for a while, and Tina moved an hour away from them. But she soon began visiting them, often for several days at a time. I see the same pattern of breakups and makeups with Meme, Paul, and Tina that I earlier saw with Tina, Matthew, and Meme.

I know Tina has suffered guilt over the way she treated Steven while he was in her care. She may also feel the same guilt that mothers who give their children up for adoption often feel. I myself have suffered guilt over mistakes I've made with my son, but I chose to talk to others about my mistakes and found new courses of action to prevent those mistakes from happening again. I have had to forgive myself. I have also had to face the reality that my son has found it difficult to forgive me. That is something I have to live with. I had to accept the fact that Matthew was his own person, with his own personality, and I had to let him go emotionally. Attending Al-Anon meetings helped me find my sanity and serenity regardless of what Matthew did or didn't do. Apparently, Tina feels no one will be able to understand her problems or feelings. Rather than do anything to change the course of her life, she seems to be allowing drugs and alcohol to consume it.

When Matthew was four years old and Mary, my therapist, encouraged me to consider letting someone else raise him, she was making a proper suggestion. Mary had no more knowledge about ADD than I did, but she did know that alcoholism hurts children, and they can become angry. Matthew was visibly hurting and angry; we just didn't understand why. Having prayed to my guardian angels since early childhood, I believe they have always helped me hold to my conviction that my son's best chances at life would be if he stayed in my care. Mary's suggestion came at a time in my life when I was vulnerable and unsure of myself. Throughout my life, and especially during the roughest times, my guides have assured me that I made the right choice.

I do not condemn Tina for choosing to turn Steven over to someone else. In fact, I think she made the most compassionate decision she could make for him. Although she was unwilling to make any changes in her life to become a better mother, she knew Steven's life was at risk if he continued living with her. I hope that someday she can forgive herself and, in fact, congratulate herself for making a wise decision. Every day, emergency rooms are filled with children who have suffered abuse and neglect from parents who have not made the courageous decision that Tina made.

Throughout the years, she has resisted every attempt made by others to get her the therapeutic help she needs. She has been able to manipulate men into "caring" for her, taking on her grievances, and becoming her spokesmen when her behaviors needed explaining. Her condition has progressively worsened. When she was in her late twenties, she was medically revived from a drug overdose, but she still refused to consider making changes.

As a society, we openly express sorrow and helplessness for those who are sick with any kind of *physical* illness. We pray for them, we cry at their funerals, and we express pity for families left behind. Although few of us understand the diseases that consume and ravage the bodies of those we love, we have compassion for those who are suffering. At the same time, however, we are often quick to condemn those who are *sick of mind or soul*. Just as we have little understanding of physical illness, we seldom understand the torment of those suffering from mental and emotional illness, including addictions.

It is easy to get sucked in by someone whose illness is not visible. We think all they need is someone to love and understand them. But people with addictions or mental illness are good at manipulating us into giving them what they want. We can be left feeling used, abused, and hopeless, and we eventually wash our hands of them when we recognize that we've been manipulated. They then move onto the next person who will try to love and help them.

If we saw someone fall down and hurt an ankle, we'd say, "You better see a doctor." The ankle might not be broken, and the doctor might only wrap it in an Ace bandage, but few of us are qualified to make a medical diagnosis. Doesn't it make sense to direct someone with a possible mental disorder to an appropriate clinician to be examined and evaluated for appropriate treatment? Why do so many of us feel qualified to help those suffering mental illnesses? Why do we think we're better than mental health professionals? I think the most compassionate thing we can do is to tell people who are mentally ill or addicted that their problems are beyond our abilities and they should seek appropriate professional help. Until more people understand that they are not helping these individuals but, in fact, hurting them by continuing to let their illnesses go untreated, few sufferers will get real help. Those who accept the help of experienced professionals, on the other hand, will have choices of pathways from self-destructive behaviors. The finest compassion is often to let go with love and stop killing with kindness.

Shortly after Matthew's relationship with Tina dissolved, he met and fell in love with Trudy, who is the woman he wants to spend the rest of his life with. After more than a year of dating, they married, and their wedding was the first time I'd seen my son happy enough to walk with a bounce in his step. Trudy has a daughter named Maegan, who is three years older than Steven. When Matthew and Trudy first married, they felt that after three years they would be in a living situation that would enable them to take Steven back. Initially, Matthew's home environment was stable enough that we had no concerns about Steven spending overnighters with his daddy, which he still does occasionally. Benjamin's and my new stepgranddaughter now spends more overnighters at our home. Steven loves having Maegan at his home. She's a good companion for him, as she's still young enough to want to shoot hoops with him, run through the yard, and sit on the steps and be quiet. She also takes Steven with her to the horse farm next door to pet the horses.

One day after Steven's daddy and new family visited us, Steven made the comment, "Maegan lives with Daddy." He clearly had given it some thought and didn't seem upset or jealous. He just seemed to be thinking, *Oh, that makes sense.* Although Steven has a lot of fun when he visits at his daddy's house, he appears to accept his living arrangements. There have been times, however, when he has cried the entire ride home. Lately he has been more focused on wanting to return home because "Grandpa is waiting for me." When Matthew and Trudy married, they bought a home near enough that visits could be easily arranged. Matthew's ability to stop by for a quick visit has helped Steven to understand that his dad is available to him.

With Matthew married to a woman who has sought counseling in her own life, he is getting more realistic feedback regarding his shortcomings. He seems to be learning some realistic facts about motherhood too, and his suspicious, hostile attitude toward me has softened greatly. He seems much more appreciative of my struggles and has even apologized for some of the problems he caused me in his youth. Matthew has worked hard at his relationship with his father, and seems to have accepted that it will always be less than he had hoped for.

Matthew did eventually have that medical diagnosis of ADD. This was after he and Steven had moved to our community he began to notice he was having problems interviewing for jobs. He said his mind raced and he talked incessantly during the interviews and that he couldn't stop the senseless chatter. Even though he initially took the recommended medication, however, he remains resistant to medications. For a time, he was able to control his outbursts, even without the medication, but his negativisms and anger have been returning. I wish I could write that being in love changed him, but love only changes everything in fairy tales. For Matthew falling in love was only a temporary fix. He will eventually be facing another opportunity to make deep personal changes which may ultimately bring him some peace and serenity. He may also choose to close all doors, as he has in the past. I am going to hang onto the belief that he loves Trudy enough that when push comes to shove, he will do whatever he has to, to save his marriage.

When he and Trudy were first dating, and it became apparent that their relationship might become serious, I asked Trudy, "What is wrong with you? Matthew is so angry. He doesn't always talk nice. You have a young daughter to think about." She claimed that for their first three months together, Matthew did talk to her in an angry, degrading fashion. She told him she would not tolerate his disrespectful behavior. If he wanted to continue in a relationship with her, he had to treat her with the respect she asked for. Since their marriage, he once made the mistake of trying to talk to me in his typical disrespectful manner, but I expect I won't be treated with disrespect anymore. It's not that Matthew is being controlled by a powerful woman. He was given a choice of treating others with respect or going on his way. He made his choice and has been, for the most part, happy with it. Old issues have a way of resurfacing, however, and until he confronts them, they will continue to cause problems for him.

Matthew's resumed parenting of Steven is probably not going to happen. On a weekend when Trudy was at a work conference and Maegan was with her father, Matthew invited Steven to spend the weekend with him, just the two of them. I learned that Matthew quickly fell back into his old habits of neglect by slipping in a video for Steven to watch while he napped on the sofa. When I confronted Matthew, he protested, "Well, how many times do you think I can keep watching the same video over and over? God! It's boring!" It never dawned on him to take Matthew to the children's park one block away or to actually spend time doing something with him. Benjamin and I had already accepted the fact that Matthew would not become responsible enough to take his son back. What was so distressing for us was acknowledging that we could not depend on Matthew for even a weekend, should we need a safe place for Steven to stay while we attended to other business. If Trudy or

Maegan were not home to care for Steven, we did not feel safe leaving him alone with his father. Benjamin and I have since sought help through Social Services to have a respite worker available to provide quality care for Steven when we need to be away or need more help.

Matthew is still obsessed with his conspiracy theories regarding our government. But Trudy doesn't want to hear about them, and they seem to be able to live with that. I think that is a healthy compromise.

Our world is filled with varying cultures, beliefs, religions, laws, governments, and personalities. Regardless of what each person's beliefs are, I hope that we can treat others with respect. I have my beliefs and my way of making the world make sense to me. I have learned from my son that my way is not necessarily going to be valid for someone else and that pushing my beliefs would be wrong. If someone likes my example and wants to take what works for me and weave some of it into their life, I would find that very satisfying. I expect and hope that anyone who takes a suggestion from me will find themselves making modifications and adjustments to better fit their life. These differences are what make each of us unique, intricate, and our own person. And it all begins with respect: respect for ourselves and for others.

On April 8, 2007, I read a wonderful essay in our local newspaper written by a seventh grader. She expressed herself so beautifully that I saved the newspaper, thinking it according with my thoughts about respecting others. I wanted to include her essay in Steven's story. When I contacted Briana's parents, her mother suggested I might like to use the original essay as the newspaper edited and shortened it. After reading the original, I agreed I should reprint her essay in its entirety.

# Born with Cerebral Palsy
By Briana Moore

I was born with cerebral palsy. Having CP is challenging. This paper will let you know how hard it is in my life and how it affects other kids like me. Here are some answers to some questions you might have about CP.

Cerebral palsy is a condition that affects thousands of babies and children each year. CP is not contagious. The word cerebral means having to do with the brain. The word palsy means a weakness or problem in a way a person moves or the position of his/her body. A person with CP has trouble controlling the muscles of the body.

There are three major types of CP. The first is called Spastic, the second one is called Athetoid, and the third is called Ataxic. The most common type of CP is Spastic. A kid with Spastic CP can't relax his/her muscles or the muscles might be stiff. Athetoid CP affects a kid's ability to control the muscles of the body. A kid with Ataxic CP has problems with balance and coordination.

This is a story about me. Babies are supposed to be born at 9 months; well, I was born at 6. One major problem with premature babies is a possibility of getting CP. This was the cause of mine. Because I was so premature, my brain cells weren't completely developed. I had some fluid in some of the undeveloped cells, and from that I got CP. When I was 6 years old, I had surgery called Rhizotomy. This surgery was on my spine. The doctors went in and cut some of my nerves from the spine so that my muscles would not be so tight, and so that I would be able to walk flat-footed instead of on my tip toes, which is how I walked before the surgery. The surgery was not to make me walk normal, only for me to walk better and to have more balance so I don't fall as much. I was in the hospital six weeks, and it took me almost a year to relearn to walk.

CP is something I will have for the rest of my life. There is nothing anyone can do to make me walk normal and not have CP. I will need more surgeries in the future to continue to help me walk as best I can and to keep my muscles from getting too tight. Most of my life I have walked with a walker, loft stand crutches, or used a wheelchair. I usually have AFOs too (braces for my feet) but right now I do not because they are waiting until my next surgery to make new ones. These AFOs are kind of a pain because it is hard to find shoes to fit over them and they are not really comfortable. I get a lot of blisters and sores.

CP affects me in a lot of ways, but I always think to myself, "You are lucky to have CP the way you do." I am not lucky to have CP, but a lot of people have it worse than I do, or it may affect their brain more, as in learning abilities. So that is why I say I am lucky. The one thing that bothers me the most is when someone makes fun of me because of the way I walk or when they stare at me. I may not be able to do some things most other kids can do, like skateboard, ice skate, and swim, but I still do the best I can. Some days it really can get to me, but then I try to think about what I can do and that maybe someday I can help others with CP learn to deal with their problems.

Everyone has disabilities. With me, you can see mine. I might look different. You won't catch CP from me. I am just as equal as everyone else. I think it is wrong for people to judge other people for their disabilities and differences. I think people should appreciate others for who they are inside and not on the outside. We all have something to give the world, no matter what we have been given by God. I believe there is a plan for all of us, and if we could think that way, it would help everyone get through their lives much easier.

I've reread Briana's essay several times. Every time I read it, it brings tears to my eyes, not because Briana has cerebral palsy, but because she is a beautiful child full of loving wisdom.

Steven is another beautiful child. He is a handsome boy and has no physical indications that he has a disability. It isn't until people begin interacting with him that they notice the obvious handicaps. Although he is unable to state his thoughts as eloquently as Briana does, he is unique in being able to make his needs known, and while he has difficulties in expressing his thoughts, he is able to tell Benjamin and me the things that are important to him. An example would be when he said, "Grandma, we need to go to church." How did he know what a church was? Why did he think we would go to one? I still don't quite know exactly how it was he convinced me I needed to write a book to tell his story. Steven loves books. He loves being read to and enjoys reading to us, but I'm not all that sure he could understand that people wrote the books he has. I think Briana has it right when she says, "We all have something to give the world, no matter what we have been given by God. I believe there is a plan for all of us, and if we all could think that way, it would help everyone get through their lives much easier."

Steven seems to know exactly what his plan is so far. My guardian angels have worked me through what would have been some frustrating times with him. I have been encouraged to believe that his learning to tie his shoes or snap his pants closed aren't nearly as important as what his plan calls for him to do. I tie his shoelaces loose enough that he can slip the shoes on and off without tying and untying them. I insert elastic into the waistbands of regular-sized pants so that he can slide them up and down his slender frame without unfastening them. We thus work around some of the things he refuses to do for himself.

*A Candle for the Children* evolved from our tradition of lighting a candle and praying for children at mealtime. When Steven prays that "other children find happy homes, like I did," he isn't praying for other children that have autism or mental delays. He is praying for all children who might be living in unhappy homes. He is praying for children who are scared, lonely, or hurting in any way because of neglect and abuse. I am still using the same clear glass candlestick we began with, and I don't clean off any of the old wax. It has a large base with a four-inch stem with the candle socket on the top. I use different-colored candles so we can see how many different candles we have burned. I have had to set the holder in a clear glass dessert plate because the wax around the base is now quite wide and the path of the melting wax needs more room.

It has taken me two years to write Steven's story. I would never put this much time and effort into writing a book if I weren't convinced of the value of sharing Steven's story. In telling this story, I have tried to include areas of our lives that were accepted as normal but were distorted and in need of change. I have tried to include suggestions and encouragement for others to make changes that might improve their lives. Change is difficult, but God will always give us the courage to face new challenges. Steven would not be praying for other children to find happy homes if he didn't think his prayers would be answered. I am absolutely honored to have been given the privilege of participating in Steven's life and contributing to his destiny. Benjamin and I joyously share our gift from God and our inspiration, which has arisen from the power of one child, one candle, and one prayer.